The ISTANA

The arcaded verandah lends shade and shelter while ensuring thorough ventilation. Suspended from the ceiling of the verandah at regular intervals are bell-shaped white opaline glass pendants that impart a touch of muted elegance.

The ISTANA

THIRD EDITION

CONTENTS

09 Foreword

10 The History

42 A Tour of the Istana

120 A Palace for the People

164 Acknowledgements

165 Image Credits

166 Bibliography

168 Index

FOREWORD

The Istana marks its 150th anniversary this year, in the same year that Singapore is also commemorating its Bicentennial. This is a good moment to reflect on how far we have come as Singaporeans, and how the Istana's evolution reflects our shared history as one people.

From the building's hybrid design and the historic events that have taken place within its walls, to the way the grounds serve as a living record of Singapore's botanical and trading heritage, the Istana embodies Singapore's rich multicultural tapestry and longstanding identity as a regional hub.

Over the years, the Istana has received many distinguished foreign leaders and hosted many significant state events. It is also the site of Singaporeans' collective memories, where many outstanding contributors to our society have been honoured and recognised. Since the first Open House in 1960, the Istana has also been opened to public five times a year, attracting tens of thousands of visitors each time.

More recently, the Istana has played host to many community groups at picnics and garden tours. We have also invited the help of dedicated volunteers to guide visitors, help tend the gardens, and organise activities for the disadvantaged.

I am glad that, over time, we have made many beautiful memories here at the Istana. This book tells its story and the many people who are a part of this story. I hope the book will inspire more to appreciate the Istana's place in the heart and history of Singapore.

Halimah Yacob
President of Singapore

THE HISTORY

The British Union Jack still flew from the central tower of Government House during the twilight years of colonialism after the Japanese Occupation.

1822: THE FIRST GOVERNMENT HOUSE

Although Stamford Raffles, an administrator of the British East India Company, is regarded as the founder of modern Singapore, the total period of time he actually spent on the island was quite brief. His longest – and final – stay in Singapore occurred in 1822, lasting some eight months. During this time, he commissioned the construction of a dwelling that eventually became the first Government House, the precursor of today's Istana.

More than two years after first landing in Singapore in 1819, Raffles returned to the island for a last visit in October 1822. He arrived from Bencoolen (now Bengkulu City, Indonesia), where he had served as the Lieutenant Governor. In poor health, he wanted a home conducive to recuperation, and settled on a site on Bukit Larangan (present day Fort Canning). The hill lay within the increasingly bustling township that had grown up along the Singapore River, and was free from the fevers and dysentery of the rural areas, while its elevation ensured cooler temperatures.

The spot also had a rich history – it was believed to be the seat of the ancient kings of Singapore. Bukit Larangan means Forbidden Hill, and this name may have originated from a

Above: Sir Stamford Raffles, who founded Singapore in 1819, had his home at Government House. It was sited on Forbidden Hill and the slight elevation was thought to make the air cleaner and more congenial to his weak health.

Opposite: The first Government House took in a wide vista from its elevated position and overlooked the original St Andrew's Church, then without tower or spire.

royal practice of forbidding commoners to ascend the hill. Its northern slope was purportedly the burial place of Iskandar Shah, one of these kingly figures. In a letter, Raffles mused that "if [his] bones must remain in the East, they would have the honour of mixing with the ashes of Malay kings".

Following the arrival of the British in Singapore in 1819, Resident William Farquhar had planted a flagstaff flying the British flag on Bukit Larangan, partly to dispel rumours of ghosts and hauntings. Raffles' bungalow was sited close to this flagstaff, and it was designed and constructed by George D. Coleman, a young Irish architect.

GEORGE D. COLEMAN

Coleman became a consequential figure in Singapore's early architectural and urban development. As an architect, he was responsible for iconic buildings such as the Armenian Church and the Old Parliament House (now The Arts House). As the first Government Superintendent of Public Works, he constructed North Bridge Road and South Bridge Road. Singapore's Coleman Street and Coleman Bridge are named after him.

Above: The view from the top of Bukit Larangan (Forbidden Hill) overseeing Boat Quay and the old harbour.

Opposite: Southern central Singapore in 1833 as captured on a map based on a survey by George D. Coleman shortly after he was appointed Superintendent of Public Works and Land Surveyor. The Irish architect also designed the first Government House, where Sir Stamford Raffles lived.

Building commenced in the last week of December 1822, and a mere fortnight and $900 later, the bungalow was completed. It was 100 feet wide and 50 feet deep, and had rough plank walls and a thatched roof of attap palm fronds.

Reviews of the new dwelling were mixed. Some praised its picturesque surroundings and panoramic view of the town's Commercial Square (later renamed Raffles Place and still the heart of Singapore's financial district). Others felt it was cramped and ramshackle, comparing it unfavourably to grander establishments owned by some of the island's European inhabitants.

Raffles left Singapore for good in 1823, barely five months after moving in. John Crawfurd, who succeeded Farquhar as Resident, moved in, and undertook some renovations – the first of many subsequent repairs, refurbishments and additions made by Singapore's colonial administrators. In 1836, this building became the Government House when the centre of administration for the Straits Settlements shifted from Penang to Singapore, but plans and petitions for a more presentable alternative continued to recur.

The fate of this Government House was only sealed in 1859. Two years earlier, a mutiny against British rule had erupted in the garrison town of Meerut, India, and spread to other parts of the country. This turn of events underlined for Singapore's colonial authorities their need for a more robust defence against threats both foreign and domestic. The latter might include unrest sparked by local pirates, Chinese secret society members, and Indian convicts.

In this context, the sweeping view from Bukit Larangan became a strategic advantage for military fortifications. In 1859, the first Government House was demolished. The site was renamed Fort Canning (after Charles John Canning, who had served as the Governor-General of India during the quelling of the 1857 Indian Mutiny), and became home to seven 68-pounder cannons facing seawards.

1869: A NEW HYBRID EMERGES

In 1867, Singapore became a Crown Colony as a part of the Straits Settlements, which also comprised Melaka and Penang. This meant that the Colonial Office in London now controlled its administration, rather than the government of British India. Harry St George Ord became the first Colonial Governor of the Straits Settlements, and put plans for a new official residence into motion.

First, he found a site – a little over 100 acres of a former nutmeg plantation, belonging to the estate of merchant Charles Robert Prinsep. The undulating plot was approximately 40 metres above sea level, and bounded by

Colonel William Farquhar was appointed Singapore's first Resident shortly after its founding by the British and he ran the island in Sir Stamford Raffles' absence.

Top: Paintings from the 1830s to 1840s depict views of the hill on which Government House was built. The top left image shows the perspective north of the Singapore River and Presentment Bridge (c. 1822, the first bridge built over the Singapore River, also known as the Monkey Bridge). The top right image captures the original Armenian Church (erected in c. 1835–1836) and on its right the Christian burial ground where early Europeans and Chinese Christian settlers were interred.

Bottom: Raffles described the view from the location of his future house, which included such sights as St Andrew's Church and the bay in the distance, as "of unequalled beauty and interest" in a letter to the Duchess of Somerset. Such a view is envisaged in the 1852 painting.

The Istana 18

Artist's impression of early Singapore showing the Singapore River and town centre. Beyond the river is the old harbour (Johnston's Pier area).

Orchard Road to the south, Cavenagh Road to the west, Bukit Timah Road to the north, and Mount Sophia to the east. It had excellent views of the town and the harbour, and was close to Commercial Square.

John Frederick Adolphus McNair, the Chief Engineer at the Public Works Department, drew up plans for a new Government House to be built on this site, and a foundation stone was laid in July 1867. But the project met some hurdles. Based on his first set of blueprints, McNair had estimated a cost of $100,000 for land, furnishings and landscaping. The Legislative Council accepted this budget, but this proved to be insufficient when the final approved architectural plan called for a much larger building than originally intended.

A painting capturing the activities that took place in and around the Padang. Wealthy residents would travel on horseback or in carriages.

The Istana 20

Opposite: By the time Sir Harry St George Ord assumed office as the first Colonial Governor of Singapore in 1867, Singapore was already a thriving colony with a tree-lined esplanade and a cricket green by the seafront.

Below: In the early 1900s, the southern borders of Government House abutted Orchard Road, a tree-lined artery into town with the occasional bullock cart trundling by at a slow pace, a far cry from the bustling shopping belt it would become.

JOHN FREDERICK ADOLPHUS MCNAIR

McNair has been described as Singapore's most important architect of the late 19th century. In addition to Government House, he oversaw the construction of St Andrew's Cathedral, and designed the former Empress Place Building (now the Asian Civilisations Museum). Having picked up photography, he facilitated Singapore's first official use of photography in his role as a supervisor of prisons, training convicts to use the camera and photographing prisoners in case of escapees. Members of the public even visited the jail to have their photographs taken.

Orchard Road, Singapore.

In 1869, McNair and Ord asked the Legislative Council for more money for the building, citing manifold reasons. The site's subsoil had turned out to be more brittle than expected, for instance, and would require a granite overlay. An infectious disease had affected many of the government-owned bullocks working the brick kilns, so more were needed. With Prince Alfred – Duke of Edinburgh and second son of Queen Victoria – slated to visit Singapore at the end of the year, the building had to be ready to host him, complete with all the bells and whistles fit for royalty.

To strengthen his case, Ord noted that even with the requested increase in funds, the new Government House would be less costly per cubic foot than public buildings such as the Court House and Town Hall. He also stressed that it would not be extravagant in ornamentation.

The request was ultimately approved, but the perception of poor management did not escape public criticism. An editorial in the *Singapore Daily Times* expressed some incredulity at the proffered justifications for a bigger budget, and an article in Hong Kong's *China Mail* described the project as extravagant. Taking a more positive tone, though, was the *Straits Times*, which opined: "Far better to have a handsome memorial of extravagance to stare us daily in the face than a memorial of folly in a half-finished or even badly-finished work."

One way McNair reduced the costs of the project was to use over 3,000 convicts, who were paid little or nothing for their labour. Brought in from various territories held

The construction of the new Government House, which took two years and was completed in 1869 after a budget overrun, was a process that incited much controversy and triggered a flurry of heated letters to the local press, mostly describing the project to be "as errant a piece of extravagance as ever was palmed off upon a helpless colony".

THE GUARDIAN OF THE HOUSE

After President Ong Teng Cheong took office in 1993, he began to research the Istana's history, and came across an academic thesis that mentioned the existence of such a statue. He was eager to retrace artifacts that were significant to the Istana's cultural heritage, and a stores officer informed him that a statue of a *mandor* (a Malay term for supervisor) in an Istana storeroom bore a striking resemblance to the description of the "Guardian of the House". The statue had been repainted in the 1900s and resembled a clean-shaven Malay man, and this was possibly an affectionate homage to a principal gardener who was popularly addressed as Mandore. During the restoration process, the statue's original layer of paint was revealed, and it depicted an Indian man with a moustache and beard.

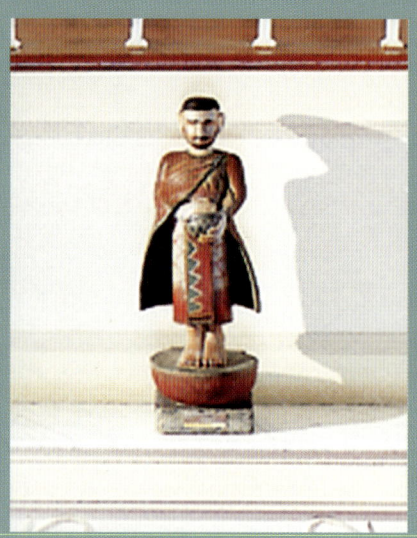

The "Guardian of the House", once believed to have been worshipped by the convicts who helped build the Istana.

under the British Empire, these men had abilities that local labourers at the time did not possess, and they became the draughtsmen, stonemasons, carpenters, painters, and welders who created the new Government House. From operating the kilns that fired the bricks for the building, to producing architectural details onsite and making detailed joinery for doors and windows, their skills and labour were critical to every aspect of construction.

In today's Istana, a wooden statue known as "the Guardian of the House" serves as a vivid reminder of these artisans. Placed on a ledge above a stair landing, the statue is believed to have once been worshipped as a spiritual benefactor by the convicts who constructed the building. It was recovered from a storeroom and restored in the 1990s, and the bowl it holds may be a symbolic container of the Istana's blueprints.

Public opinion about Government House changed after it was completed, with the once-hostile press expressing approval of the building.

The new Government House was completed in 1869, and it was a rich and unique hybrid of Eastern and Western influences – a cultural confluence that would define Singapore in the years to come.

With its classical features and stately symmetry, the three-storey building had a neo-Palladian style that characterised many British state buildings of the period. But it also had the signature layout of a traditional Malay house, and was built to respond to the local context of heat, humidity and lashing rainstorms. Features such as deeply recessed verandahs and louvred windows sought to provide shade and shelter from tropical weather, and the building's façade faced the direction of the sea to better receive prevailing winds.

Some furnishings and materials were ordered from Europe, but the bulk reflected regional resources and know-how. The internal walls were plastered with chunam, a special stucco derived from Madras that was manually smoothened after drying to a glistening whiteness by polishing with rock crystal. Stone and granite were sourced from Pulau Ubin, lime from coral atolls around Singapore, paving marble from neighbouring regions such as Java, and wood from the sawmills of Johor.

This Government House soon became a hub for local and visiting high society, earning praise for its lush gardens and hosting glittering soirées. During their visit in 1882, Prince Albert Victor and his brother Prince George of Wales (later King George V) noted many details for posterity, including the uniforms of the liveried staff, which comprised white tunics, scarlet and gold-laced belts, and broad, flat scarlet hats.

For the first 50 years of the building's existence, most staff, from grooms to gardeners, lived on the grounds. In 1913, barracks for 10 to 12 Sikh guards were added, and their presence would prove to be useful when a mutiny broke out at the Alexandra Barracks on February 15, 1915. Dissatisfied with their conditions of service and fuelled by anti-British sentiments, members of the 5th Indian Light Infantry Regiment wounded and killed officers and civilians as they fanned out across the city.

European women and children sought refuge at the Government House, whose Sikh guards were stationed all over the grounds in anticipation of an attack. By the next morning, even the Government House was considered to be no longer safe, and the refuge-seekers were sent to an ocean liner docked at the port.

The mutiny was quelled after a few days, with help from the marines of Japanese, French and Russian warships. While this eruption of unrest may have been brief, more turmoil would soon follow as the tumultuous 20th century unfolded.

World War II had begun in Europe in 1939, and soon expanded into Asia. In late 1941, the Japanese air force

The History 27

The Duke and Duchess of Cornwall, seated in a horse-drawn carriage, made their way through a crowd of well-wishers and curious onlookers when they visited Singapore, c. 1900.

No less than $6,500 was spent on the interior furnishings, mostly from England, which was a princely sum for the time. The house enjoyed a system of underground drainage and roof cisterns supplying water to the bathrooms.

started to bomb Singapore. In the days leading up to the Japanese invasion on February 15, 1942, there was intense shelling near Government House, and staff were instructed to hide in the cellar. They stayed there for days, surviving on stocked rations by candlelight.

On February 13, Shenton Thomas, who would be the last Governor of the Straits Settlements, moved from the Government House to the Singapore Club. The following day, from that more secure location, he recommended immediate surrender to the Japanese forces. Thomas became a prisoner of war during the ensuing occupation.

Meanwhile, the Government House staff tried to escape via a tunnel connected to the cellar, but Japanese soldiers discovered the escape hatch and pushed grenades into the tunnel. Those who survived carried the bodies of the deceased with them as they fled to houses along (Kampong) Java Road.

The Japanese renamed Singapore as Syonan, and the Government House became a base for its Southern Expeditionary Forces. In March 1943, Supreme Commander

During the Japanese Occupation, Count Hisaichi Terauchi, who led the conquest of Southeast Asia, became the main resident of Government House along with other Japanese officers. He only did minimal redecoration of some rooms to give them a Japanese flavour.

Hisaichi Terauchi moved in. Japanese soldiers brought the Government House staff back to the building, where their duties remained largely unchanged. They wore the same uniforms they had sported during the British regime, and the new occupants of the building made only minimal adjustments to its décor. Terauchi even slept in the same bed that had been used by Thomas.

Still, life had changed irrevocably. The staff had to learn Japanese so they could understand orders. Along the boundaries of the estate, British and Australian prisoners-of-war buried dead Japanese soldiers and repaired the fences that had been damaged by shelling. A new bomb shelter was built on the grounds. In 1943, a reception and garden party was held for Japanese Prime Minister Hideki Tojo.

Two years later, the tides of war turned again. The Japanese surrendered; the British returned. The Straits Settlements were dissolved, and Singapore became a Crown Colony in its own right. In the immediate post-war years, war veterans and civilians who had supported Allied interests were honoured with a variety of accolades at ceremonies of investiture held at the Government House.

Life in the building seemed to return to its old rhythms, but with the tenor of a final refrain. In 1952, a grand ball was held here in honour of the visiting Duchess of Kent, and her son, the Duke of Kent. The following year, the house was a central venue for the festivities celebrating the coronation of Queen Elizabeth II. In 1958, it hosted a garden party to mark the queen's birthday – this was one of the last social events at the Government House under the colonial regime, and one where "solemnity was the keynote", according to a *Singapore Free Press* report.

In 1948, William Hare, the Minister of State for Colonial Affairs, had held a press conference at the Government House, stressing the sincerity of the British government in developing self-governance in its colonies. By 1959, Singapore had begun to embark on full internal self-government.

Opposite: Examples of how different rooms were furnished when Sir Franklin Gimson and his immediate successor, Sir John Nicoll, resided in Government House.

The Istana 32

The interior of Government House during the tenure of Sir Franklin Gimson from 1946 to 1952. Sir Franklin took over the military administration of Singapore from Lord Louis Mountbatten who accepted the Japanese surrender in 1945.

THE CANNON ON THE GUN TERRACE
After the war, a 105mm Japanese gun was presented to Singapore by Louis Mountbatten, then the Supreme Allied Commander of Southeast Asia. Now placed on the Istana's Gun Terrace, the 3,730kg cannon was likely deployed by the 15th or 33rd Army of the Imperial Japanese Army, and serves a reminder of this painful chapter of history.

Today, the Gun Terrace is set amidst lush landscaping that is characteristic of the Istana grounds.

1959: A NEW CHAPTER BEGINS

On December 3, 1959, Yusof Ishak — a former journalist and the chairman of Singapore's Public Service Commission — became the new Yang di-Pertuan Negara, a ceremonial position created to replace the British Governor. Government House was given a new name — Istana Negara Singapura, or Palace of the State of Singapore.

The new symbols of this fledgling state were introduced at the Istana. Cutlery, crockery and crystalware that bore the British crest were replaced with those embossed with Singapore's new crest. Local fare replaced British food on the menu (with First Lady Puan Noor Aishah's signature recipes becoming particular favourites).

SYMBOLS OF SELF-GOVERNANCE

Unveiled in December 1959, the State Coat of Arms comprised a shield with a white crescent moon (symbolising a young nation on the ascent) and five stars (standing for the ideals of democracy, peace, progress, justice, and equality). The lion supporting the shield on the left represented Singapore; the tiger on the shield's right symbolised historical links with Malaysia.

A year later, the Presidential Crest was created. Its shield represented the head of state's role as the defender of Singapore's Constitution, and it was coloured red for universal brotherhood and equality, and white for virtue and purity. On the shield, a lion bears a stalk of laurel — a representation of victory and glory for Singapore.

The President's Personal Standard, a red flag with a crescent moon and five stars at its centre, was adopted in 1961. This flag is flown from the highest point of the Istana's main building.

The Presidential Crest.

Most notably, concerted efforts were made to open up the Istana for the people. Under the British regime, regional Asian aristocrats from sultans to maharajahs had been guests at Government House events, and invitations to members of the local upper-crust Asian community had increased beginning in the 1930s.

Still, few regular members of the public had been given a chance to visit. That changed on January 1, 1960, when the Istana held its first open day. The Ministry of Social Affairs provided swings, slides and seesaws for children, while adults strolled the grounds, enjoying live music played by the Police Band, and recorded tunes piped from public address vans by the Ministry of Culture.

The President's Standard, which resembles the Singapore flag except it has only red as a dominant colour, is flown whenever the President is in the Istana and taken down when he or she is on leave or abroad. This is a legacy from the British tradition in which the monarch also has a personal Royal Standard.

A bird's eye view of the Istana showing it nestling among groves of mature trees in 1969, when Singapore's first President, Yusof Ishak, was head of state. President Yusof served from 1965 to 1970.

CREATIVE FLOWERING

President Yusof lived in Sri Melati, a more private building on the grounds of the Istana. An avid gardener, he cultivated orchids, some of which ended up gracing the centrepieces during official dinners.

The first Asian household manageress of the Istana, Jean Leembruggen, also had a knack for striking floral arrangements. She cut lilies from the Istana's lily pond after sunset, when their petals had curled into budlike shapes. These blooms unfurled when exposed to illumination in the dining room, much to the guests' delight.

One of the people who interviewed Leembruggen for this job was Prime Minister Lee Kuan Yew, then in his 40s. She was later told by her predecessor that Lee had remarked after the interview that he thought she was rather young for the job, to which she responded: "He's rather young to be a Prime Minister too!"

On June 2, 1960, a banquet was held at the Istana to mark the first anniversary of the attainment of internal self-government and the birth of the State of Singapore. In his opening address, Yusof said: "Differences of race, religion, creed and even political differences have not prevented our people from joining together to celebrate the first anniversary of the success of a democratic government in a self-governing state."

Following the separation from Malaysia in 1965, Singapore became an independent nation and the Istana Negara Singapura was abbreviated to the Istana. Yusof was no longer Yang di-Pertuan Negara, becoming the first President of Singapore. That meant, among other things, that he could select a serving officer from Singapore's armed forces to serve as his aide-de-camp (ADC) — the person who oversaw ceremonial duties and the staff who kept the Istana running as a household.

The first ADC was Captain Winston Choo of the Singapore Infantry Regiment, whose new post meant he had to postpone his wedding for a year, as the regulations of the time required the ADC to be a bachelor who would reside within the Istana.

Singapore's first President, Yusof Ishak, and his wife, Puan Noor Aishah, sustained the tradition of hosting garden parties at the Istana in recognition of those who had contributed to charitable causes. On this occasion in 1966, helpers of the visually impaired were honoured.

Today, staff no longer live on the premises, and distinguished guests are no longer lodged here during their visits. These are just some of the many changes have been introduced at the Istana, including the addition of a Japanese garden, a marsh garden, and four ponds to the grounds, and a surely welcome evolution of staff uniforms into more comfortable attire.

But the vision of the Istana as a place for the people has remained constant since that first open day. Open House days are now held five times a year, with tens of thousands of Singaporeans and visitors streaming into the grounds for such events. The Istana is also the venue where the nation's best and brightest receive scholarships, and where Singaporeans from all walks of life are celebrated for outstanding achievements and important contributions in diverse fields. It has been a symbol of colonial authority, a place of refuge during crises, and stands as a proud survivor of war. Most importantly, 60 years since it became a palace for the people, the Istana has also become a cherished repository of Singaporeans' collective memory.

A TOUR OF THE ISTANA

Flowerbeds form part of the formal Front Lawn of the Istana. Many of the flowers are cultivated in the Istana's own nursery for decorative and landscaping purposes.

State guests arriving by car will get their first glimpse of the Istana before being escorted into the foyer.

ARCHITECTURE

The Istana Main Building sits on top of a 40m-high hill that was once described as "the most commanding spot on the island". On a clear day, one used to be able to glimpse the Indonesian islands and the hills of Johor, Malaysia from this spot. These days, the view is very different – the skyscrapers of the central business district now take centre stage on the horizon. Just outside the Main Gate of the Istana domain, the hustle and bustle of traffic and pedestrians along Orchard Road is further testament to how much Singapore has developed over the past 150 years.

Gazetted together with Sri Temasek as a National Monument in 1992, the Istana embodies the history and evolution of this fast-changing city state. The Main Building's architecture reflects its colonial roots, with hallmarks of a classical British style that was widely adopted for civic buildings beginning in the 18th century. The 28m-tall central tower is topped with a slate mansard roof, and flanked by colonnaded wings, each terminating in pediments. The frontage employs a classic Palladian hierarchy, with a row of Doric pilasters, architraves, cornices and arches at the base, followed by Ionic columns, a continuous cornice and balustrade on the next tier, and Corinthian columns and dormer windows on the highest tier.

A Tour of the Istana 45

This architectural style had begun to evolve when the British brought it to India, and the Main Building illustrates how it also adapted to Singapore's tropical context. Besides a layout that echoed that of a traditional Malay house, with the entrance porch leading to rooms on either side, the Main Building borrows from other features of regional architecture. It rests on dwarfed arches and piers that elevate it over a metre above the ground — much like houses built on stilts, this enables better air circulation and ventilation. Deeply recessed verandahs, hooded openings and overhangs, and louvred windows and shutters also help to temper heat and reduce glare.

The building was well appointed from the start, with a foundation of 15 feet, and the front block sitting on granite plates. Underground drainage was installed, and roof cisterns supplied water to the bathrooms. In 1869, when the building was completed, a princely sum of $6,500 was spent on furnishings, which were mostly imported from England. Subsequent governors added their own decorative touches, in the form of furnishings, china, cutlery, carpets, decorations and linen.

Periodic renovations over the years helped to ensure the Main Building kept up with the times and always presented its best face to the public. In 1913, the first electric lamps were installed, and electric fans replaced the manually operated punkahs. Other modern amenities, such as a lift and a refrigerator for the kitchen, would soon make their appearances in the years that followed.

In 1914, a two-storey annexe was added to the rear of the east wing. The annexe was designed in a classical style, with features such as large casement windows and decorated plasterwork, to ensure it was in harmony with the Main Building. In 1936, a third storey was added to this annexe, to house staff accommodation and offices. The year 1940 saw $108,600 worth of repairs made, along with the addition of more rooms in the Main Building. Repairs made immediately after World War II were undertaken by

Above and opposite: While the interiors of Government House supposedly paled in comparison with the dwellings of the rich Chinese merchants of that period, its location "in the midst of a beautiful park", as characterised by the wife of the First Earl of Brassey, more than compensated for its perceived inadequacies.

VIEWING PLEASURE

A significant change during the refurbishments in 1940 was the conversion of the front porch roof into a flat terrace. Today, this terrace serves as a balcony from which one can enjoy a panoramic view of the grounds.

Japanese prisoners of war. In 1954, the addition of yet more offices and other renovations cost $182,000.

The most extensive overhaul took place from 1996 to 1998, during which original features were restored or replaced, the interiors were redesigned and a three-storey extension added. Great care was taken to retain and enhance the architectural character of the building while also sprucing it up.

For instance, modern fittings such as mechanically activated louvres and air-conditioning were introduced, and glass walls were consequently added to the external verandahs. The original flooring of white Java marble on these verandahs, which was damaged, was replaced with white granite imported from Spain. Bell-shaped opaline lights whose glass shades were mouth-blown in Austria were added, alternating with three-bladed period ceiling fans for a touch of understated elegance. New automatic sliding glass doors were installed for the front porch, paired with a new gate left open at all times as a symbolic gesture of welcome.

In 2017, the Function Lawn underwent a year-long upgrading exercise – its wooden trellises have been replaced with metal ones, and a new drainage system and lightning conductors have been installed.

Ground Floor:
Entry Foyer and Atrium

With its polished white marble floor and walls lined with Ionic pilasters and Doric columns, the foyer gives a first impression of formal grandeur, which is accentuated by the row of polished strass full-lead-crystal chandeliers on the ceiling, done in an 18th century design known as Maria Theresa.

Look a little closer, however, and you'll spot some endearing homegrown touches. The Guardian of the House takes pride of place on the landing of the foyer's central white marble staircase (which sports a deep red Axminster woven runner carpet with a flake design). The ceiling's plaster mouldings feature familiar tropical fruits. Chinese and Peranakan furniture and artefacts, such as a circular teak table of Straits Chinese design, also help to create a sense of place.

LET THERE BE LIGHT
The curving arms and glittering crystal prisms of these Maria Theresa chandeliers provide much of the illumination and adornment in the Main Building. Their metal parts are gold-plated, then encased in flat glass strips to soften their hard edges. The chandeliers are complemented by strass crystal lights fitted on the walls.

A Tour of the Istana 49

A prestige guard in the number one uniform of the Singapore Armed Forces watches over the entry foyer of the Istana.

The Presidential Crest with its wreath of orchids surmounted by the symbolic crescent moon and five stars of the national flag sits upon the entrance to the Istana Main Building.

A Tour of the Istana 53

Opposite: Columns frame the arches of the stairwell that leads up to the first floor reception area. In the middle of the white marble staircase is the "Guardian of the House" wooden statue.

Top left: An I Wayan Bendi painting commissioned by the Istana in 2005. In the work, the artist makes humorous and insightful comments on the social, political and cultural environment of Singapore.

Top right and bottom: Above the lift lobby is a stained glass skylight in the design of a floral medallion that allows natural light through the ceiling.

The atrium, which is illuminated by the sunlight streaming in through a stained-glass skylight 18.5 metres above, also showcases pieces from the Istana Art Collection. Besides sculptures, paintings and photographs by Singaporean artists such as Iskander Jalil and Russel Wong, there is also one artwork by a foreign artist in the collection; a painting by Balinese artist I Wayan Bendi depicts an intricate Singapore cityscape and is currently displayed in the atrium. The piece was commissioned by President SR Nathan in 2005, and created after the artist spent a week in Singapore.

Opposite: Artwork by local artist Chua Mia Tee of five Presidents and their respective Cabinets which once adorned the Sheares Room. President Ong commissioned the portraits to document Singapore's early years of nationhood.

THE ISTANA ART COLLECTION
There are about 100 pieces in this collection, which is also part of Singapore's national collection. The Istana Art Collection Advisory Committee, created by President Ong Teng Cheong in 1994, guides the acquisition and commissioning of artworks for the Istana Art Collection, with the goal of reflecting developments in Singapore's art history and cultural achievements. Pieces from the collection are rotated every 18 to 24 months for display at the Istana, and that's because (even with air-conditioning) the building is not considered to be a controlled environment conducive for the long-term display of art. Of course, this also means repeat visitors have a chance to view a greater variety of artworks.

In fact, the Istana has been inviting Singapore's artists to document its milestones since the early years of independence. In 1966, sculptor Lim Yew Kuan and painter Chan Khun Yew were commissioned to create a bust and oil painting respectively of President Yusof Ishak. President Ong also commissioned artist Chua Mia Tee to create a painting of Singapore's first five Presidents, each surrounded by their respective Cabinets.

Reception Hall and State Room

The entry foyer leads to the Reception Hall on the left and the State Room on the right. Both are used to welcome visitors during formal occasions, and were designed and decorated with that purpose in mind.

The Reception Hall has a light colour scheme, with touches of blue in its Persian carpet and orange damask draperies adorning the floor-length French windows. The latter hue also appears in the upholstery of the antique Louis XIV chairs. A 2017 triptych by batik painter Sarkasi Said, titled *Istana Garden*, is displayed here.

In the State Room, a rich maroon red is the dominant colour. A small carpeted and curtained stage, positioned between two niches, is used during official presentations. The State Room is used for the inauguration of Presidents, the swearing-in of the cabinet, as well as other investitures and award presentation ceremonies.

Above: With swagged valances, arched fanlights and draperies in a woven damask fabric, the Reception Hall is an elegant setting for guests.

Opposite: The State Room is designed to host official presentations and seat a large number of people. It is illuminated by neat rows of chandeliers with sprays of faceted crystals trailing from golden silk robe stems. Sandwiched between two niches cradling floral displays is a small stage draped with velvet curtains, which is often used for official presentations of awards.

THE QUEEN VICTORIA STATUE

The State Room was called the Victoria Room during colonial times. Its name derives from a statue of England's Queen Victoria, which was commissioned in 1889 by Singapore's Chinese community leaders to mark the monarch's Golden Jubilee. Created by Polish-born sculptor Emanuel Edward Geflowski, the 1.8m tall white marble statue was presented to the colonial government and placed in this room until Singapore attained self-government in 1959. In 1994, the statue was recovered from a National Museum store in Jurong, restored with the help of specialists from the Victoria and Albert Museum in London, and placed in a gazebo at the Istana's Lily Pond. In 2015, it featured in an exhibition at the Peranakan Museum, and subsequently displayed at the National Gallery Singapore, before returning to the custody of the National Heritage Board.

Banquet Hall

Also on the ground floor is the 293 sq m Banquet Hall, a space that used to house kitchens and mechanical and engineering workshops. Now, it is used for formal dinners. Paved in beige marble inlaid with a trellis design, the doors, windows, entablature and pilasters here are replicated from the original rooms on the ground floor. Dress curtains and large gilded mirrors add a touch of grandeur, as does the imposing 2.35m-wide Maria Theresa-style candelabra in the centre of the ceiling, which weighs 220kg. The mini-stage here is used for official presentations, and it sits inside an arched alcove with a trompe l'oeil landscape depicting the Istana grounds, painted by Singapore artist Lim Kay Hiong. A secondary porch on the side of the west wing allows guests a more private way to access the Banquet Hall.

Top: One of the oversized gilded mirrors within the Banquet Hall reflecting the rows of crystal wall sconces.

Bottom: On the mini-stage along one side of the Banquet Hall sits a small arched alcove, forming a window into a trompe l'oeil of the Istana garden.

The 220kg candelabra-type chandelier in the Maria Theresa style, with a dramatic drop from the centre of the coffered ceiling in the Banquet Hall, measures nearly 2.35m in diameter.

The cavernous Banquet Hall which was converted from former kitchens and machine rooms is the largest hall in the Istana and provides ample space for guests and dignitaries to mingle while enjoying refreshments.

Above and opposite: The Banquet Hall is a hive of activity on evenings when state functions are held on the premises. On this particular day, President Ong Teng Cheong extends a warm welcome to a crowd that includes then Prime Minister Goh Chok Tong and Mrs Goh.

A Tour of the Istana 63

First Floor: Reception area

The 350kg Maria Theresa-style chandelier here measures 3.6m by 1.7m, which makes it even more massive than the one in the Banquet Hall. Indeed, it took four specialists three days to install this fixture. But size isn't everything – the two much smaller chandeliers over the half-landing of the grand staircase have their own claim to fame, being restored Viennese antiques that were first gifted by the last emperor of Austria to the third Duke of Buckingham.

Lighting of aristocratic provenance notwithstanding, the first floor generally has a more homely atmosphere compared to the more formal ground floor. Instead of marble, for instance, the floors here are mostly made of thick Nyatoh wood.

Below: One of the two restored antique chandeliers of Viennese origin, the oldest of their kind in the Istana, in the main reception area.

The reception area on the first floor is lit by a massive chandelier, a Maria Theresa model weighing 350kg. It casts light over a formal seating arrangement comprising a mixture of Chippendale and Gainsborough-style furniture.

Recessed verandahs encircle the perimeters of the rooms on the first floor and these have now been glassed in and air-conditioned. Handpicked items of furniture are placed in comfortable configurations.

Blue and white vases of Ming extraction, porcelain lampstands, mahogany armchairs with cabriole legs and tracery of an embossed wisteria motif provide aesthetic relief.

East Drawing Room

Designed to look like a traditional parlour, this room features sofas upholstered in a soft golden hue, a mahogany drum table, and a Pakistan Ardabil carpet in navy blue.

Behind a vintage hand-painted chinoiserie screen is the Yusof Room, named after Singapore's first President. Here, visitors can dine at circular, 19th-century English-style tables while seated in Chippendale-style mahogany chairs. Artefacts of note here include a bust of President Yusof, and a pair of antique Chinese vases that date back to the Qing Dynasty Kuang Hsu period of the late 1800s and early 1900s.

Like the other public rooms on the first level, the architectural relief and entablature of the East Drawing Room have been restored. To maintain the grace of symmetry, the row of chandeliers is in complete alignment. The chinoiserie screens separating the East Drawing Room from the Yusof Room can be seen in the background.

Opposite: In the Yusof Room, visitors can dine in the reduced formality of two circular, 19th-century dining tables. A mahogany display cabinet along one wall adds to the homely feel.

Above: A bust of President Yusof Ishak, Singapore's first head of state, sits in the room named after him.

Left: A vintage chinoiserie screen with birds and flowers against a dark background divides the East Drawing Room from the Yusof Room.

Above: The West Drawing Room is separated from the Sheares Room in the background by a chinoiserie divider.

Opposite: The West Drawing Room is dominated by Louis XIV chairs in dark leather and sofas upholstered in rich damask.

West Drawing Room

This room is somewhat more formal that the East Drawing Room, with damask sofas and Louis XIV chairs in dark leather.

The Sheares Room, named after Singapore's second President, Benjamin Sheares, lies behind a multi-panel screen depicting a traditional Oriental scene. It also functions as a dining and meeting room. Here, a boat-shaped, 18th-century English-style mahogany dining table stands on an Ishfahan carpet that took 10 years to weave. The latter is based on a Shahabhasi design that dates back to the 16th century. The bust of President Sheares displayed here was sculpted by artist Lim Yew Kuan in 1999.

The Sheares Room, named after Singapore's second President, has a long dining table that provides a more formal setting than the Yusof Room.

The President's Lounge

Taking pride of place on the first floor is the President's Lounge, which has a beautiful view of the Front Lawn. Here, a Louis XVI beech dining table with fleur de lis marquetry is surrounded by a dozen Imperial chairs of mahogany palm veneer, sitting on a square floral Persian wool carpet woven by a famous Tabriz master. Rosewood furniture lacquered in black and inlaid with mother-of-pearl adds accents of refinement. The President's office is on the third floor.

Above: The entrance to the President's Lounge is enhanced by a decorative artwork of a horse (left). Decisions about the affairs of the state are made in the quiet respite of the President's office on the third level of the Istana (right).

Opposite: The President's Lounge looks out onto the Ceremonial Plaza and the Front Lawn. It is distinguished by a strass chandelier with multiple prongs capped by opaline white shades and hanging from one of 16 recessed coffers on the ceiling.

SRI TEMASEK, ISTANA VILLA AND THE LODGE

Besides the Main Building, the Istana domain also consists of Sri Temasek, Istana Villa and The Lodge. The latter was built on the site of the former Sri Melati (which means fragrant jasmine), which served as the residence of President Yusof Ishak from 1959 to 1970. In the early 1970s, Sri Melati had to be demolished due to damage caused by termites.

Sri Temasek

This two-storey building was constructed along with the Main Building in 1869. A blend of Western and Eastern styles, it is most notable for the fretwork of its exterior timber arcade and interior stairway. Originally built to house the Colonial Secretary, the building became the official residence of the Prime Minister after independence, and is now used for various functions and ceremonies. Discussions for Singapore's merger with Malaysia took place here, and the separation agreement was also signed here.

Opposite: The staircase leading to the second level of Sri Temasek also features delicate fretwork.

Below: The delicate fretwork that adorns Sri Temasek's timber arcade shows an intercultural blend of Eastern and Western decorative motifs.

View of the restored Sri Temasek from the driveway.

Opposite: The wide verandahs of Sri Temasek act as a buffer between the building and the rays of the hot tropical sun.

A Tour of the Istana 81

The Istana 82

From the verandahs of Sri Temasek, one has splendid views of the surrounding grounds, including the Istana Villa.

The Istana 84

The Istana Villa was built as the home of the aide-de-camp who was required to stay in it. It has also served as a guesthouse for visiting dignitaries.

The Istana Villa

Built in 1908 to house the Governor's aide-de-camp and later the Private Secretary, this building is designed in the black-and-white architectural style that was adopted for many colonial homes in Singapore. In 1958, it became the Attorney-General's house. Subsequently, it was used for small functions, and as a guesthouse for notable guests, such as Chinese Premier Deng Xiaoping, US President George Bush and Malaysian Prime Minister Mahathir Mohamad.

In 2009, a sculptural work by Cultural Medallion recipient Han Sai Por was installed outside the villa. Titled *Transformation Series 2*, this artwork is an exploration of "what comes to take the place of nature after man's act of changing the landscape", and comprises evenly spaced sandblasted granite nodes on stainless steel bars.

The Lodge

This single-storey building was built in 1974, on the site of the former Sri Melati. The Lodge served as the home of President Devan Nair from 1981 to 1985, and was subsequently President Ong Teng Cheong's office.

Opposite: The single-storey lodge was built in 1974 and served as the home of Devan Nair, Singapore's third President. His successor President Ong Teng Cheong made it his office while the Main Building was being renovated. It stands on the site of the former Sri Melati.

Sri Melati was the residence of Singapore's first head of state. Built in 1869, it provided President Yusof Ishak with homely comforts while simultaneously ensuring close proximity to his office at the Istana Main Building.

Part of the Function Lawn with the centre fountain which is activated when there are official functions and on Open House days.

THE GROUNDS

Just as the Istana's architecture, art and artefacts serve as a record of the nation's culture and history, its sprawling grounds nurture Singapore's flora and fauna, and embody its Garden City ethos.

Landscaping was an essential element of Government House from its inception. Laurence Niven, the Superintendent of the Agri-Horticultural Society's gardens, established a nursery on the grounds and cultivated a wide variety of trees and shrubs. Successive residents of Government House added to its grounds over the years, with improvements such as more nurseries to supply cut flowers. At their height, these nurseries had approximately 20,000 potted plants, with some flowers winning awards at the Singapore Flower Show in the 1950s. Various sporting facilities have also come and gone, including a croquet lawn, bowling green, and a golf course.

Former governors such as Sir Charles Hugh Clifford and his wife started the practice of cultivating fruits and vegetables on the grounds, for the purpose of supplying Government House's dinner table. Thanks to Lady Clifford, the first crop of cauliflower was grown in Singapore here, in 1938. During the Japanese Occupation, the Istana gardens grew high-carbohydrate foods such as maize, tapioca, sweet potato and yam, to tide its occupants over during the lean war years.

The Istana grounds were administered by the Director of Botanic Gardens until 1966, when this responsibility was assigned to the Private Secretary to the President, and later the National Parks Board (NParks). After independence, the Istana gardens began to reflect the environmental values that were to guide the development of this newly conceived Garden City. Preserving biodiversity was one such value, as was the importance of maintaining green public spaces to create a better quality of life for all. The prudent use of natural resources also became particularly important for a country without a self-sufficient water supply.

FROM GREENS TO LAWNS

The Istana's now defunct golf course traces its roots back to the early 1900s, when Governor Sir Arthur Young, an enthusiastic golfer, acted on earlier suggestions for a few holes to be included in the grounds. This was eventually expanded into a nine-hole course. In 2012, the greens of carpet grass were converted to lawns of cow grass, which are easier to maintain.

In that spirit, ponds were added to the Istana grounds over the years to serve as reservoirs, and the Istana plants are watered with water from these ponds, rather than with potable water. That means when dry season hits the island and pond water levels drop, most plants here have to wait for rainfall to regain their lush appearance.

NParks continues to oversee the grounds today. A team of 15, led by Group Director for Fort Canning Park & Istana, Wong Tuan Wah, works from the Istana, with support from their NParks colleagues when needed. The grounds are now home to 261 species of over 10,000 trees and plants, as well as 90 bird species. Its onsite nursery has 5,000 pots at the ready for various landscaping and decorative needs, and more are sourced from NParks' main nursery in Pasir Panjang.

The wide range of edible plants here — from tropical fruits to local greens — are harvested by the NParks team and presented to the kitchen staff, who use these ingredients in salads, desserts and other delectable gastronomic showcases for homegrown flavours. Similarly, the flowers grown here are used to bring colour, fragrance and beauty to both outdoor landscapes and indoor arrangements.

The strategic location and undulating terrain of the Istana estate affords occasional glimpses of the soaring edifices in the financial district.

The Istana sits on what used to be a nutmeg plantation and despite its transformation into the office of the leaders of Singapore, it has not lost its connection to nature with its vast repository of flora and fauna.

The Istana 94

Trees within the Istana grounds include 100 mature trees (with girths of more than 4m). There are also five heritage trees (girth size 5m and above) — a Rain Tree, a Buddha Coconut, a West Indian Locust, a Binjai, and an Asam tree. The oldest tree on the grounds is a Tembusu tree believed to be over 150 years old, and it is among the living treasures on the grounds to have been fitted with a lightning conductor for extra protection.

Indeed, as more of the Istana's trees are getting on in years, tree inspection and management have been intensified. New methodologies and equipment are being used to help NParks better understand these trees' internal structures and detect decay. New trees are also planted regularly, and many of these are native tree species that take a long time to mature but will grow tall when they do.

Opposite: The rich horticultural heritage of the Istana domain is exemplified by the wealth of plant species including the Sage Rose, *Ixora javanica*, Heliconia, *Codiaeum variegatum*, *Lantana camara*, *Pseuderanthemum reticulatum* and Vanda Miss Joaquim. Such variety ensures a palette of colours during blossom time.

Right: In a landscape where natural greenery is comfortably reconciled with the artifice of man-made gardens, the gnarled roots of trees add a dimension of antiquity.

A Tour of the Istana 97

Above and opposite: The Istana grounds not only host a wide variety of birds, including some that stop over during their annual migration, but different species of wildlife such as butterflies, squirrels, dragonflies and monitor lizards can be found here as well.

Naturally, the Istana's fecund protected grounds are also a great home for wildlife — butterflies, dragonflies, fish, squirrels, bats, flying foxes, monitor lizards and snakes can all be found here. Notably, it is a gazetted bird sanctuary where migratory birds such as raptors, Japanese Sparrowhawks and Yellow Wagtails stay when they leave their native climes at the onset of winter. Local species such as starlings, bulbuls, and kingfishers are also present, along with more exotic species like the Black-crowned Night Heron and Collared Owl.

THE SINGAPORE HORNBILL PROJECT

The Oriental Pied Hornbill is a local species once thought to be extinct before it was spotted again in 1994. The Singapore Hornbill Project, spearheaded by Marc Cremades and Ng Soon Chye, was a breeding programme for these birds, and the Istana was a part of its success. In 2008, Jurong Bird Park donated two hornbills to the Istana. Named Sada and Lili, the birds were encouraged to breed and lay their eggs in artificial nesting boxes installed on the grounds, and they did, producing two chicks. Today, there are about a hundred hornbills in Singapore, and some return to the Istana during their breeding season from November to April.

To enjoy the flora and fauna at close range, members of the public can visit the Istana grounds five times a year during Open House Days. In 2014, President Tony Tan even launched an Istana Garden Walk app to help visitors learn more about the grounds. Developed by Temasek Polytechnic, the app enables visitors to scan QR codes at different points in the Istana domain, thus allowing them to take an informative self-guided tour.

An aerial view of the Front Lawn that has been divided into parterres and encircled by pergolas and columnal shrubs. A certain structured formality is imposed on the immediate vicinity of the Istana Main Building.

Istana Park and Istana Heritage Gallery

The Istana Park and the Istana Heritage Gallery give visitors a year-round chance to learn a little more about these historic grounds and get a sense of what they are like.

The park, which faces the Istana Main Gate, opened 1996, to bring the grandeur of the Istana grounds onto Orchard Road. It features a Festival Arch, designed by Japanese architect Ren Matsui, and a reflecting pool.

During Open House days (which are held during Chinese New Year, Labour Day, Hari Raya Puasa, National Day and Deepavali), the central decorative field in front of the arch features a seasonal plant display that celebrates these festive occasions. To mark the Open House on National Day, for instance, the NParks team works with volunteers a month in advance to prepare plants with red and white blooms, and they take two days to get the display ready.

The park is also the site of the Istana Heritage Gallery, launched in 2016 by President Tony Tan as an engagement platform where the public can learn more about the Istana's history, as well as the role of the Presidency.

> **A TRIO OF GUARDIANS**
> The original Guardian of the House statue presides over the Istana Main Building from its perch on the grand staircase, but two replicas of it exist, both commissioned by the Indian Heritage Centre (IHC). One replica can be found at the IHC on Campbell Lane, which traces the history of the Indian and South Asian communities in Southeast Asia. The other replica is displayed in the Istana Heritage Gallery.

The Main Gate

Believe it or not, access to the Istana used to be fairly informal. A proper entrance to the domain in the form of cast-iron gates with a Flemish arabesque design was only installed in 1931, and a Visitors Book Room at these gates allowed guests to sign their names before entering. (This is now known as the Centre Gate, and marks the division between the upper and lower reaches of the domain's Edinburgh Road driveway.) The iron fence surrounding the Istana domain was only built during the Japanese Occupation, by Australian prisoners of war.

Today, the main entryway to the Istana is the Main Gate along Orchard Road, which was also built in around 1931. One of the most popular sights here is the Changing of Guards ceremony.

Opposite left: A different perspective of the amply shaded sentry posts that passers-by may not be immediately acquainted with. The Istana Park can be seen across the road.

Opposite right: Two pairs of cast-iron gates in an elaborate Flemish design stand inside the Istana grounds.

CHANGING OF GUARDS

The first Changing of Guards ceremony took place in 1969. It was performed by the Singapore Armed Forces Guards Unit (SAFGU) based on the ceremony at England's Buckingham Palace. The responsibility was handed over to the Singapore Armed Forces Military Police Command in 1980.

The half-hour ceremony now takes place on the first Sunday of every month (except during July and August), at 5.45 pm. It involves 36 guards, two guard commanders and a military band. The incoming unit marches up Orchard Road, and the outgoing unit marches from the Guard House within the Istana grounds. They converge outside the Main Gate, line up in four columns, and a simple handover ceremony takes place while the band plays martial tunes. The ceremony ends with a Rifle Precision Drill.

By 1985, the Changing of Guards outside the Main Gate, featuring the pomp of precision drills executed by the military police accompanied by the music of the military band, had become an entrenched tradition with throngs of onlookers.

Edinburgh Road

Once inside the gates, visitors will see the 1km-long Edinburgh Road that winds through the grounds. Named after the Istana's first VIP guest, the Duke of Edinburgh, the path is flanked by majestic Rain Trees whose branches form a beautiful canopy. Other verdant vegetation lining this road includes Wild Cinnamon plants, ferns, Wild Pepper bushes and yellow blooms of the Sanchezia.

Above: Today, the Centre Gate serves as a landmark between the upper and lower reaches of Edinburgh Road.

Opposite: The leafy arms of Rain Trees weave a tapestry of green and form a natural canopy along Edinburgh Road while giant ferns nestle in their boughs.

The Swan Pond

Constructed in 1968, this body of water near the Main Gate lies to the left of Edinburgh Road and got its name from the pair of white mute swans gifted by the Zoological Society of London. (The pond's current pair of swans hails from the Netherlands). In 2012, seven Lesser Whistling Ducks from Jurong Bird Park joined the pond. Swifts, kingfishers and mynahs can also be spotted here. Measuring about 150m long and 42m at its widest point, the pond has two levels divided by a weir, and is the largest of the six ponds within the grounds. This site used to be a cemetery, where resident workers were buried when they passed away.

Although swans can be spotted at the Swan Pond, as befitting its name, different bird species can also be seen quenching their thirst from its waters on many evenings.

The Japanese Garden

Completed in 1967, this miniature Japanese Garden lies just beyond the Centre Gate, and its pine trees and bonsai-like Dwarf Bamboo create a sense of zen. A small wooden bridge allows for a bird's eye view of a small ornamental pond filled with Japanese carp.

Below and opposite: With its cluster of pines and bamboo looking over a quaint little pond accentuated by miniature stone lanterns, the Japanese Garden is one more variation in a compound of myriad delights.

Orchid Garden

Just outside the Istana Villa is an Orchid Garden celebrating Singapore's national flower. The brainchild of Mrs Mary Tan, wife of President Tony Tan, this garden was planted in 2015 to mark Singapore's Jubilee, and has since been expanded at the suggestion of President Halimah Yacob.

Orchid cultivation has a long history at the Istana, and different varieties can be found growing in other spots within the grounds, as well as adorning the interiors of the buildings. The practice of naming specially cultivated hybrid orchids after VIPs started in 1956, and the NParks team at the Istana works with the National Orchid Garden to maintain these heritage orchids, and make sure guests with namesake orchids can enjoy viewing these blooms when they visit.

Ginger Garden

Introduced in 2016, this garden near the Istana Villa comprises a variety of gingers used for culinary and medicinal purposes in Asian culture, as well as plants in the ginger family.

Spice Garden

Mrs Mary Tan got the idea for this garden after visiting the Community in Bloom show gardens at the Singapore Garden Festival in 2014. It was launched in 2015 with the help of volunteers, and features about 30 species of spices and herbs such as chili, ginger, lime, pandan and lemongrass.

The following year, ingredients from this garden were used to create the Istana's signature drink, the Istana Harvest. The Istana Harvest Sorbet, based on ingredients from the garden, was then introduced and presented by President Tan and Mrs Tan in 2017 to commemorate Singapore's 52nd birthday.

Spices are a big part of the Istana's story, since it sits on the site of a former nutmeg plantation. In 1989, as a nod to these roots, nutmeg trees were reintroduced to the grounds upon the suggestion of founding Prime Minister Lee Kuan Yew.

SEAT OF MEMORIES

Placed across the grounds are 14 benches that speak to a different aspect of Singapore's history. These are made from the backless wooden benches of the former National Stadium, and pay homage to the much-loved sporting venue that was torn down in 2010.

President Tony Tan and Mrs Tan joined Community in Bloom volunteers in the Spice Garden in 2015.

Other spices that helped trade flourish in early Singapore, such as cloves, are also planted here, making it a living repository for the country's mercantile and botanical history.

The Lily Pond

Built in 1951 on the site of a former fern and orchid house, this rectangular pond is filled with the water lilies that give it its name, and is fringed with semi-aquatic plants such as the Cypress Papyrus, Canna, Thalia and Wild Yams. Fan Palms, ginger plants, Ornamental Bananas and Heliconias adorn the paved walkways surrounding the pond.

The Istana 112

Above and opposite: Visitors can enjoy the seclusion of the Lily Pond after descending several flights of steps.

Right: Before being moved out in 2015, the statue of Queen Victoria was sheltered under a gazebo at the end of the Lily Pond.

A view of the Ceremonial Plaza and entrance to the Main Building of the Istana.

The Front Lawn

Spanning 18,200 sq m, this lawn was redesigned during the 1990s, and is terraced into three tiers, each descending in height as one moves from the Main Building.

The uppermost tier, outside the Main Building's front porch, incorporates the Ceremonial Plaza and the Upper Lawn (parterre), where honoured guests alight from their vehicles and are welcomed to the Istana. Foreign leaders on state visits and dignitaries would be greeted formally by a welcoming ceremony complete with a guard of honour.

Before the redesign, guests were welcomed at a tarmac plot at the side of the Main Building. Now, the plaza's flat, paved surface provides space for military parades and band performances, while four flagpoles provide a sense of occasion. A carefully cultivated plot of flowers also delights the eye, with blooms of yellow, red and orange chosen to create a sunny atmosphere.

Beyond these sunny blooms a flight of steps leads to the the Function Lawn. With an elegant black marble fountain in its centre, this lawn can host garden parties and dinners for up to 1,500 guests. The colour scheme here is a more serene blue, white and purple, courtesy of plants such as the Glory Bush, Music Notes, and Cat's Whiskers. On the perimeter, semi-circular trellises are covered with Bauhinia and Bread Flowers. This section ends in a viewing terrace, which not only overlooks the Lower Lawn, the final tier of the Front Lawn, but also looks out into the distance at the Singapore skyline; a view that has changed so much over the last 150 years and will no doubt continue to change.

A Tour of the Istana 117

The Istana, captured in its full glory, shows the descending tiers of the Front Lawn which ends in a semicircular balustrade and a pair of stairs that lead gracefully to a terrace of flowers.

The Istana   118

The Main Building of the Istana is the perfect backdrop for souvenir snapshots during Open House Days.

A PALACE FOR THE PEOPLE

SOCIAL HUB

The Istana has had no lack of distinguished visitors. In fact, back when it was known as Government House, its first VIP guest was the Duke of Edinburgh, and his impending visit in 1869 even became part of the justification for increasing the building's construction budget by $20,000, to provide for amenities such as doorbells and stables that would make the premises more fit for royalty. The picturesque Rain Tree-flanked Edinburgh Road that serves as the Istana's driveway is named after this first guest.

A few years later, when Sir Andrew Clarke became the Governor of the Straits Settlements in 1873, he and his wife turned Government House into a social hub for European visitors stopping over in Singapore en route to China. For those with large retinues, additional accommodation was found at Hotel d'Europe. Originally located at Hill Street, it was then known as one of the finest hotels in Southeast Asia (along with Raffles Hotel), and – adding to its cachet – was even perceived as an annexe to Government House since it hosted so many sojourners who were invited to Lady Clarke's soirées. The doors of that grand old hotel were shuttered in 1932 and the building was later demolished, making way for the Supreme Court.

A Palace for the People 123

Calling at Government House quickly became an essential part of visiting foreign dignitaries' schedules. The Sultan of Selangor, Abdul Samad called on the Governor in 1890 with a large entourage of courtiers and attendants in tow.

To welcome these guests, the Government House often staged elaborate festivities. In 1882, brothers Prince Albert Victor and Prince George of Wales attended a fancy dress ball thrown in their honour, which saw 4,000 paper lanterns strung from trees, and the building's façade lit up with gas jets. The princes even climbed to the summit of the house to enjoy the enchanting illuminations. Others were entranced by the grounds' lush greenery. During her stay in 1876, English botanical artist Marianne North wondered how other guests could be content with the usual English pastimes of lawn tennis and croquet when there were such fascinating tropical plants at hand to study.

A considerable number of staff was naturally required to maintain a household that could graciously host such guests on a regular basis. The employees of Government House lived on the grounds, and some of their job titles reflected the times. For example: there were punkah pullers, who manually operated the framed cloth fans that kept residents cool before electricity was introduced, and syces who were responsible for taking care of the horses. With the advent of newer technology came newer jobs, such as telephone operators.

For many years, these staff members were pretty much the only Asians at Government House, apart from the occasional emperor or sultan who came to call. That began to change during the 20th century, albeit slowly. In 1918, in a ceremony held at Government House, Tan Teck Neo, known for her charitable works, became the first Chinese woman to be conferred the title of Member of the British Empire.

At the helm during the transitional post-World War II years was Sir Franklin Gimson, who would be remembered as a slow but meticulous administrator by his staff, a sizeable community in 1951 judging by this group portrait.

HOME GROUND

In the 1920s, some Government House staff shifted to quarters outside the grounds, at Mackenzie Road and McNair Road. But many continued to live here, along with their families, and there was even a kindergarten on the grounds for the young children of staff. It was only in the 1970s that staff quarters were phased out completely.

In 1918, Tan Teck Neo, also known as Mrs Lee Choon Guan, was the first Chinese woman to be conferred the title of Member of the British Empire at a ceremony officiated by Sir Arthur Henderson Young.

TAN TECK NEO

The daughter of Chinese businessman Tan Keong Saik, who has a road in Chinatown named after him, Tan Teck Neo married Lee Choon Guan, a prominent business and community leader. In 1915, she founded the Chinese Ladies' Association, which is now known as the Chinese Women's Association, one of the most longest standing philanthropic organisations in Singapore. During World War I, she was a Red Cross volunteer in England. Later in life, she became the patron of Singapore's Po Leung Kuk, a society for the protection of women and girls.

When Sir Laurence Guillemard became the Governor of the Straits Settlements in 1920, Asian members of the local elite became regular attendees at Government House functions. By 1935, when a garden party was held in honour of King George V's Silver Jubilee, the guests in attendance included those of many different races and ethnicities. The following year, lawyer and community leader Song Ong Siang became the first Chinese man in Malaya to be knighted, receiving the Badge of Knight Commander of the Civil Division of the Most Excellent Order of the British Empire, in Government House's grand ballroom.

During the Japanese Occupation, Supreme Commander Hisaichi Terauchi moved in, and the building also housed other senior Japanese army officers, as well as chefs flown in from Japan to prepare meals for the new occupants. Guests during this period included Japanese Prime Minister Hideki Tojo.

After the war, events at the Government House resumed their British character, but there was evidence of greater inclusivity. In 1952, guests at a garden party held in honour of the visiting Duchess of Kent and her son, the Duke of Kent, included 30 social welfare workers, half of whom were Asian. In 1953, to celebrate the coronation of Queen Elizabeth II, 3,500 pupils from both English and vernacular schools were invited to the grounds to enjoy film screenings, puppet shows, and acrobatic performances. Six days later, 48 fisherfolk from the Southern Islands of Pulau Bukom Kechil and Pulau Seraya toured the premises, and met the Governor at a reception held in Government House.

Sir Laurence Nunns Guillemard threw open the doors of Government House to members of the Asiatic community.

SONG ONG SIANG

A recipient of the prestigious Queen's Scholarship in 1888, Song was a top student who studied law at the University of Cambridge, and became the first Chinese barrister admitted to the Singapore Bar. He was one of the community leaders who set up the Singapore Chinese Girls' School, and one of the earliest members of the Chinese company of the Singapore Volunteer Infantry in 1901. In 1915, he became the first Chinese man in Malaya to be promoted to the rank of captain.

A Palace for the People 127

Garden parties on the Front Lawn of Government House were a regular feature in the social calendar of the Governor and his wife in the mid-1950s. These occasions found one and all decked out in their finest.

GUESTHOUSE FOR VIPS

Until 1984, VIP guests stayed on the Istana premises, where their bedrooms used to be stocked with amenities such as Lux soap. One frequent guest was Lord Mountbatten, who favoured Annexe Room 6. Today, visitors to the Istana stay in one of the many 5-star hotels in Singapore and the Istana bedrooms have been converted into offices.

Singapore's second President, Benjamin Sheares (right), engaging Lord Louis Mountbatten, who received the Japanese surrender in Singapore at the end of the Second World War, in a serious discussion in 1976.

STATE OF INDEPENDENCE

By the time Queen Elizabeth II began her reign, a new chapter had begun for Singapore. Visitors and events at Government House during this period reflected the changing times. In 1955, a general election for Singapore's Legislative Assembly was held for the first time, and members of its Council of Ministers were sworn in at Government House. In 1958, British Prime Minister Harold Macmillan paid a visit during his 35-day tour of the Commonwealth, during which this architect of decolonisation sought a clearer picture of the local political situation.

In 1959, Singapore attained full self-governance, and Government House became the Istana Negara Singapura, and in 1965, following the separation from Malaysia, the Istana. In these fledgling years of nationhood, new symbols of sovereignty such as Presidential Crest were installed here. Just as important were the new ceremonies devised to reflect the values and dignity of Singapore.

For instance, protocols had to be developed for how staff should escort VIPs at the Istana, and how they ought to be seated during formal occasions. The presentation of credentials by ambassadors and high commissioners to the Singapore President was one such important ceremony, the particulars of which were settled on after similar protocols in various countries were studied. The proceedings for

A Palace for the People 129

Prestige guards dressed in military splendour stand at attention in the Ceremonial Plaza awaiting the arrival of official guests. Soldiers carry M-16 weapons affixed with bayonets only during the most formal of parades.

Singapore were designed to be dignified but not overly elaborate, with ambassadors driven to the Istana in a car, rather than a carriage, for example. These days, they also view a video at the Istana Villa to familiarise themselves with the ceremony before they are formally introduced to the President in the Main Building's West Drawing Room.

Visiting heads of state and other domestic and foreign dignitaries are greeted with a Welcome Ceremony held at the Main Building's Ceremonial Plaza, where they inspect a Ceremonial Guard-of-Honour. Heads of state are usually greeted by 72 guards, while the column may be smaller for other dignitaries. A state banquet often kicks off with a fanfare for a touch of formal grandeur. Even a less formal meal needs to be timed to the minute. All these little details add up to convey a full picture of Singapore's competence and graciousness.

Similarly, Istana events involving foreign guests now focus on strengthening ties between Singapore and other countries. In 1985, President Wee Kim Wee started the President's Annual Diplomatic Reception as a gesture of appreciation for the local diplomatic corps. The annual International Institute for Security Studies Shangri-La Dialogue is marked by a dinner for the delegates held at the Istana. In 2015, representatives from 18 countries were hosted to a lunch at the Istana before heading to the SG50 National Day Parade at the Padang.

President Benjamin Sheares, with Mrs Sheares beside him, welcoming Kenneth Kaunda, the Zambian President in 1971.

Bottom: A formal luncheon hosted by Puan Noor Aishah at the Istana.

A Palace for the People 131

DUTIES OF THE AIDE-DE-CAMP

The President's aide-de-camp (ADC) is in charge of overseeing ceremonial proceedings and events, and is trained in all aspects of etiquette. There are now three full-time ADCs, and they are assisted by Honorary ADCs who are senior officers from the military, police and civil defence forces.

The President's aides-de-camp pose for a group photograph with President SR Nathan after their appointment ceremony.

President Halimah Yacob undertaking a Guard of Honour inspection.

A Palace for the People 133

President Halimah Yacob in conversation with the King of Jordan, Abdullah II bin Al-Hussein, during a state banquet in 2019.

UPSTANDING YOUTHS

The Singapore President is also the Chief Scout, and Boy Scouts visit the Istana once a year during Scout Job Week to do odd jobs here. The Girl Guides similarly have a longstanding history with the Istana. In 1967, Puan Noor Aishah even hosted a campfire on the grounds for them. In 1970, the First Lady became the first Asian President of Singapore Girl Guides Association, which named an award for outstanding Brownies and Girl Guides units after her.

Other awards named after the President are also conferred at the Istana, and they celebrate outstanding individuals from all walks of life, including teachers, social workers, nurses, artists, volunteers and social enterprises. The goal is to shine a unique spotlight on their varied contributions to Singapore.

The Istana opened its gates to the public in 1960. Among the diverse events that took place there was a Scouts Rally. Scouts continue to be a presence at the Istana today during Scout Job Week.

The Istana is also the site for several important award ceremonies. One is the Investiture of the Distinguished Service Order (Military), which is formally termed the Darjah Utama Bakti Cemerlang (Tentera). It is Singapore's highest military award, and honours individuals who have contributed to the forging of excellent defence ties between Singapore and the recipient's country. The Distinguished Service Order, awarded by Singapore Police Force, honours those who performed acts constituting distinguished conduct within or outside Singapore.

SOME AWARDS PRESENTED AT THE ISTANA
Since 1998: President's Award for Teachers and
             Outstanding Social Worker Award
Since 2000: President's Award for Nurses
Since 2002: Cultural Medallion
Since 2004: President's Volunteerism & Philanthropy Awards
Since 2006: President's Award for the Environment
Since 2008: Promising Social Worker Award
Since 2009: President's Science and Technology Award
Since 2009: President's Design Awards
Since 2012: President's Challenge Social Enterprise Award

The President also confers the Honorary Citizen Award, the highest form of state recognition for non-Singaporeans who have made outstanding contributions to Singapore; as well as the Public Service Star (Distinguished Friends of Singapore) Award and the Public Service Medal (Friends of Singapore) Award, which recognise senior executives who have helped to advance Singapore's economic growth.

The majority of the award ceremonies held at the Istana celebrate Singaporeans. The first President's Scholarship Presentation Ceremony was held here in 1966, to confer prestige to the nation's top students. In the following year, the first Singapore Armed Forces Commissioning Ceremonies were held here.

The President's Scout Award and the President's Guide Award are also bestowed on outstanding youths from these organisations at the Istana. These accolades used to be named after the King or Queen of England, and were renamed after Singapore attained independence. They were among the earliest awards to be presented at the Istana. Since 2005, the Istana has also been the venue for the Boys' Brigade President's Award.

Above: A group of President's Scholars share tea and conversation with President Halimah Yacob.

Opposite: Distinguished efforts in the civil service sees recognition granted to teachers and nurses with an invitation to the Istana.

A Palace for the People 137

Above: A proud recipient is conferred with the Distinguished Service Order.

Below: The Istana has been the venue for the Boys' Brigade President's Award since 2015.

Above: An Honorary ADC receives his commission and salutes President Halimah Yacob.

Below: The Cultural Medallion was instituted in 1979 by President Ong Teng Cheong (then Minister of Culture) to recognise individuals whose artistic excellence has enriched and distinguished Singapore's arts and cultural landscape. Mr Chua Mia Tee (front, fourth from right) was one such artist who received a Cultural Medallion from President Tony Tan in 2015.

Above: The Istana garden also served as a site for Deputy Prime Minister Goh Chok Tong's consultative approach when he hosted an alfresco reception for 200 professionals and business personnel in 1988.

Below: A conductor guides a group of young musicians during an Istana Open House.

Of course, one doesn't have to win an award to be a guest at the People's Palace. National Servicemen are invited to the Singapore Armed Forces Garden Reception, while public service officers attend a gathering here during Public Service Week every year. Members of the law profession attend the Chief Justice's dinner banquet held at the Istana, which kicks off the legal year. There are also events for business leaders, seniors, athletes, families and myriad other communities.

President Wee, a former journalist, was known for scouring the newspapers for civic-minded acts, and then inviting these everyday heroes to the Istana for tea. President Ong, a music lover, requested a Steinway baby grand piano for the West Drawing Room, and invited talented young musicians to perform during dinner parties. Various school bands and members of the Singapore Symphony Orchestra now play at Istana Open Houses.

STATE GIFTS

Another popular attraction for Open House visitors is the display of state gifts in the Banquet Room. There are over one thousand such gifts from foreign dignitaries in total, and each Open House features a different selection of 70 to 100 state gifts.

Above: Ornamental plate presented by HM King Mohamed VI of Morocco to President SR Nathan in 2005. Moroccan ceramics are characterised by their bold colours and designs.

Right: Qatar presented this ornament in gold and silver. It features two symbols of Qatar, the Arabian oryx and the palm tree.

Left: Japan's rich culture is represented in this geisha doll dressed in a hand-painted kimono.

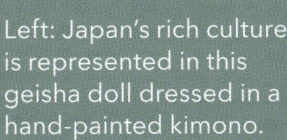

Left: The President of Chile presented this elaborate yerba maté tea cup and bombilla straw. The straw is specially designed to prevent the drinker from ingesting the tea leaves.

Right: Bencharong jar from Thailand. The word "bencharong" means five colours and refers to the process of hand painting enamel over glazed ceramic.

A MORE OPEN HOUSE

While the 1990s overhaul of the Istana spearheaded by President Ong was undertaken primarily to improve the condition of the building, the renovations led to an unanticipated but happy outcome — new fire safety measures for the Main Building meant that members of the public visiting the Istana during Open House events could now visit parts of the building that had previously been inaccessible.

Over the years, other efforts have made these Open House days more engaging. In 2002, President SR Nathan led a collaboration with the Singapore Art Museum and the National Heritage Board for the Istana Art Event, which featured art competitions for children and other art-related activities. This has since become a much-loved feature of Open House days.

The Istana Art Event has become a favourite part of Open House days since it began in 2002.

The specially curated exhibition at the Istana Heritage Gallery captures the Istana's transition from being the Colonial Governor's House to its present role as the Office of the President.

In 2013, President Tony Tan introduced guided tours of the Istana Main Building for Open House visitors, which are led by volunteers from the Preservation of Sites and Monuments Board. The following year, the National Parks Board (NParks) and the President's Office collaborated on offering Nature Guided Walks during Open House days, with visitors led through the grounds by volunteer guides trained by NParks. The nominal fee that visitors pay for these tours are donated to charities supported by the President's Challenge. Volunteers also began engaging visitors at the Istana Heritage Gallery when it opened in 2016.

Volunteers continue to contribute to the Istana. In 2017, President Halimah Yacob launched the Volunteer Gardeners@Istana programme, inviting those who were passionate about gardening to volunteer in the Istana's gardens. These volunteers can sign up to come to the Istana for three days each month, and they don't even need to be well versed in gardening. The NParks team based in the Istana will guide them in their tasks, and the scheme has proven to be very popular, attracting 170 volunteers so far, including many retirees.

A dance group from Singapore Management University entertains President Tony Tan and members of the public during the Labour Day Open House in 2017.

Snacks and stories keep children entertained during Picnic@Istana events, a popular initiative that has been running since 2017.

As part of her community engagement programme, President Halimah Yacob also launched two other platforms to make the Istana more accessible for Singaporeans. One is Garden Tours@Istana, whereby seniors and their caregivers are invited to tour the grounds and Main Building. The other is Picnic@Istana, which treats underprivileged children or those with special needs to picnics along the banks of the Swan Pond.

These initiatives are a reflection of President Halimah's longstanding passion for social causes, which has led to her becoming the patron of organisations such as Club Heal (which supports persons with mental health issues) and the Ain Society (which supports cancer patients).

With much experience in working with underprivileged groups, there was an awareness that the regular Open House events might not be conducive for people such as the elderly, who may not be able to navigate crowds safely if they are using wheelchairs, for instance. The garden tours and picnics are thus designed to help these visitors have an optimal experience at

For those who are less mobile, specially organised garden tours provide a unique opportunity to enjoy the Istana.

the Istana, which they are usually visiting for the first time.

Engaging and diverse activities, such as puzzle-solving and drawing for the children, are always planned for such visits, yet there is always one common highlight for all these events: President Halimah always joins the participants. She has read storybooks to children by the Swan Pond, and chatted with seniors about their impressions of the Istana, and is always keen to engage with these visitors.

Each garden tour and picnic has about 40 to 60 participants, which have included those from beneficiary organisations of the President's Challenge. Other organisations have also approached the Istana to be a part of these initiatives. As a result, garden tours have been organised for hospice patients and long-stay patients of the Institute of Mental Health. Feedback has been very positive across the board. Parents who accompany their children for the picnics, for instance, have shared how much they appreciate the bonding experience, while many seniors said they never expected to be able to visit the Istana in their lifetimes.

Above: Providing greater accessibility for less mobile visitors is a key factor in recent initiatives such as Garden Tours@Istana.

Below: An NParks volunteer guide imparts some wisdom to volunteer gardeners.

It is all smiles for children invited to a picnic at the Istana.

PRESIDENT'S CHALLENGE

Initiated by President SR Nathan in 2000, the President's Challenge invites people from all walks of life to help the less fortunate and build a more caring and inclusive society. It currently has over 50 beneficiary organisations. In 2012, President Tony Tan expanded the platform beyond fundraising, to also include volunteerism and social entrepreneurship. In 2018, President Halimah Yacob announced an Empowering for Life Fund to support vulnerable groups through skills upgrading, capacity building and employment.

President SR Nathan overseeing the launch ceremony of the President's Challenge in 2000.

President Halimah Yacob also involves youth volunteers in her community engagement activities and within the Istana. As the patron of Youth Corps Singapore, President Halimah has rallied its members to contribute to society, and one way they responded to her call was by spearheading a garden tour event at the Istana for elderly participants, which even included a session of wheelchair yoga on the grounds.

Behind the scenes, vulnerable communities are also getting the chance to use the Istana as a valuable learning ground. In 2017, seven Secondary 4 students from the Association for Persons with Special Needs (APSN) Katong School became Istana interns, picking up cooking and horticultural skills from the Istana's kitchen staff and NParks curators to help prepare them for gainful employment.

The initiative was first pitched by Mr Han XuanChou, a Culinary Trainer and Job Coach in APSN Katong School, who was an Istana chef during President SR Nathan's tenure. The internship experience "helped the students gain invaluable work experience, confidence and skills", said a spokesperson for the school. "This meaningful engagement promotes social integration and awareness of people with special needs, building a strong foundation and moving forward to an inclusive society."

A DREAM COME TRUE

In 2017, President Halimah read a *Straits Times* feature about Paul Simon, a 26-year-old chef with a mild intellectual disability who worked at the Rasa Sentosa Resort and Spa. This story was part of the newspaper's celebration of persons with disabilities in their respective areas of work, to mark the International Day of Disabled Persons. In his interview, Simon said his dream was to one day cook for President Halimah. A month later, this dream came true when she invited him to cook a three-course meal at the Istana. Simon's menu for the special occasion: mango salsa salad, chicken briyani (with the gravy based on a cherished family recipe), and sweet corn sago. The president and the chef enjoyed the last course together while sharing a friendly chat.

Opposite: In 2017, seven Secondary 4 students from the Association for Persons with Special Needs (APSN) Katong School became Istana interns, picking up cooking and horticultural skills from the Istana's kitchen staff and NParks curators to prepare them for gainful employment.

Subsequently, to mark the Istana's 150th Anniversary in 2019, APSN Katong School students were invited to submit artwork to be used on the packaging for cookies made with ingredients from the Istana gardens, and sold during Open House events to raise funds for the President's Challenge. The students created artwork based on the grounds' flora and fauna, and five students' creations were ultimately selected. One of them is Nabilah Tsabitah binte Mohammad Zakir, who shared: "I felt excited painting the Istana because it was my dream palace. I was also very happy to meet our President Halimah Yacob. My parents were very proud of me."

In fact, a whole new set of Istana memorabilia was commissioned in 2018, all featuring designs and drawings by special needs artists. These items range from keychains to fridge magnets, and all sales proceeds are donated to the President's Challenge. Some are also presented as gifts to Istana guests, helping to highlight another aspect of the Singapore story.

A Palace for the People 157

Above: In 2018, a new set of Istana memorabilia was commissioned, featuring designs and drawings by special needs artists.

Opposite: To mark the Istana's 150th Anniversary in 2019, APSN Katong School students were invited to submit artwork to be used on the packaging for cookies made with ingredients from the Istana gardens.

These efforts to showcase the talents of such groups are ongoing, and mean a great deal to the artists involved. In 2019, two residents of the HCSA Dayspring Residential Treatment Centre for abused teenage girls were invited to draw the Oriental Pied Hornbills that are sometimes spotted on the Istana grounds. Their work was subsequently featured on the President's Hari Raya greeting card. The two artists "were honoured to be able to play a part and also very touched to each receive a Hari Raya greeting card with a personalised message from Madam President," said Vivian Lim, Assistant Director of Marketing & Communications for HCSA Community Services.

Beneficiaries of The Autism Association (Singapore), or AA(S), have also contributed artwork for the design of Istana gifts. For instance, Ms Lai Zer Yinn, a student of the association's Eden Talent Development Programme for Visual Art, created artwork that was subsequently featured on an Istana porcelain plate and Istana Chinese New Year and Hari Raya packets. These items can be seen in the 2019 roving exhibition, "Our Istana: A Living Museum".

This artwork of Oriental Pied Hornbills was created by two residents of the HCSA Dayspring Residential Treatment Centre for abused teenage girls and subsequently featured on the President's Hari Raya greeting card.

"Autism Association (Singapore) is incredibly honoured to collaborate with the Istana to showcase our beneficiaries' talents. The Istana is an important partner to help rally the community to support persons on the autism spectrum and provide a platform to create an inclusive society for our special ones," said Mr Ho Swee Huat, Chairman of Autism Association (Singapore).

Zer Yinn and her mother, Madam Poon Wan Sin, were invited to attend the exhibition launch. "I am happy that AA(S) has provided my child with opportunities and experiences that help her learn, grow and maximise her potential in the visual arts. With support and recognition from the Istana of Zer Yinn's talent, I am confident that together we can create greater awareness of persons with special needs' talents that may otherwise go unnoticed," said Madam Poon.

Ms Lai Zer Yinn, a student of AA(S) created artwork that was used on an Istana porcelain plate and Istana Chinese New Year and Hari Raya packets.

Visitors to the roving exhibition also received limited-edition postcards featuring Vanda Miss Joaquim orchids painted by six TOUCH Special Needs artists from TOUCH SpecialCrafts – Jeremy Koh, Esther Lim, Cheng Chiang Yong, Annie Teo, Chen Zhiyu and Philip Wong. This engagement was a collaboration with SG Enable's (SGE) i'mable initiative, which spotlights the abilities of persons with disabilities through the works of special needs artists and artisans.

Working closely with Singapore Philatelic Museum (the appointed curator of the exhibition), SGE curated artworks drawn by these talented artists from TOUCH SpecialCrafts, who were very excited to be part of the exhibition. "It means a lot to our trainees that their talent is affirmed and that they get to interact with the public and share their passion for art," said Ms Vanessa Lam, Senior Lead, Partnership, TOUCH Community Services. "TOUCH is honoured that the works of our Special Needs trainees are showcased through this meaningful and momentous milestone of the Istana."

Among the exhibition highlights is a watercolour painting of the Istana Main Building by 11-year-old Ashley Marie Nonis, a student of St. Andrew's Autism School. She worked on the piece over three 50-minute sessions, with guidance from her art teacher Madam Rohayah Abdul Majid. In 2018,

A watercolour painting of the Istana Main Building by 11-year-old Ashley Marie Nonis, a student of St. Andrew's Autism School.

Ashley was also one of the special needs students whose artwork was featured on the National Day Parade funpack — another project in which "she was very engaged and did very meticulously", says Madam Rohayah. A week after the 2018 NDP, Ashley, and her father Nonis Brandon Mark were invited to the Istana along with other NDP participants as a gesture of appreciation. "As we reached the Istana, Ashley got very excited as it was so beautiful and to her it looked like a castle," her father recalled. "She was very happy that day, as she met and shook the hand of the President. She felt really special. It is really hard for her in everyday life, and my family would like to thank everyone for making her feel accepted and appreciated."

A Palace for the People 161

President Halimah Yacob with her husband, Mr Mohamed Abdullah Alhabshee, and Istana staff.

A projection of the Singapore flag on the Istana provides a stunning backdrop as soldiers from the SAF Military Police Command perform precision drills. This was part of a dramatic light show that wowed members of the public during the Istana 150 Commemorative Event, held on 6 October 2019.

ACKNOWLEDGEMENTS

The book you hold in your hands is the third edition of a work that has appeared in two slightly different guises before, although this is the first time the book will be made widely available to the public. All three editions share the same title, *The Istana*.

The first edition was published in 2000 and was authored by Dr K K Seet. The second edition was published in 2011 and was authored by Dr Leong Ching. Photographer Peter Mealin's beautiful images of the Istana buildings, interiors and grounds adorned the first two editions of the book, as they do now for a third time. We are grateful to these talented individuals for these past efforts; their contributions endure in this new edition.

Ms Hong Xinyi was invited to update and revise the text for this third edition, a task she fulfilled with aplomb. Xinyi spoke to many people during the course of her work, and we thank the following for their time and insights: Vanessa Lam, Jeremy Koh, Esther Lim, Cheng Chiang Yong, Annie Teo, Chen Zhiyu, Philip Wong, Rohayah Abdul Majid, Michelle Pang, Ashley Marie Nonis, Nonis Brandon Mark, Michelle Jimenez, Jesse Sie, Lai Zer Yinn, Poon Wan Sin, Vivian Lim, Han XuanChou, Nabilah Tsabitah binte Mohammad Zakir, Zunitah binte Rohani, Lim Xin Yi, Lim Jia En Tracy, and Mong Qian Hui.

We wish to reaffirm our appreciation to the various agencies, entities and individuals who have made photographic contributions to the book; the image credits on the opposite page offer more detailed recognition.

We thank all staff of the Istana, both past and present, who have helped in one way or another in the publication of this book.

Lastly, we thank the Singaporean public. This book has only been produced because of your enduring support and enthusiasm for the Istana.

IMAGE CREDITS

The photographs in this book were taken by Peter Mealin, except for those credited below.

The Istana: 35, 111, 112 (bottom), 120-121, 131, 132, 133, 134 (bottom) 136, 137, 138, 139, 140 (bottom), 142-143, 144, 145, 146-147, 148, 149, 150, 151, 152, 153, 154, 156, 157, 158, 159, 161

MITA Collection, courtesy of National Archives of Singapore: 28, 29, 31 (top right), 32-33, 39, 118-119, 124, 127, 128, 130 (top), 134 (top), 140 (top)

National Archives of Singapore: 10-11, 12, 15, 16, 21, 25, 31 (top left and bottom), 38-38, 125, 126

National Museum of Singapore: 13, 14, 17 (all), 19, 22-23, 47

National Library Board, Singapore: 18, 20

Mr Wong Tuan Wah, NParks: 96 (all), 97 (all)

Lim Kheng Chye's Collection at the National Archives of Singapore: 27

Collection of Royal Commonwealth Office, courtesy of National Archives of Singapore: 123

Mrs Jean Leembruggen: 130 (bottom)

Ms Ashley Marie Nonis: 160

Antiques of the Orient: 46

NParks: 112 (top), 113

BIBLIOGRAPHY

MANUSCRIPTS
Straits Settlements Records. 1800–1867.
Governor's Letters to Bengal. 1824–1867.
Governor's Letters to Resident Councillors. 1856–1867.
Governor's Miscellaneous Letters (Out). 1958–1867.
Governor's Miscellaneous Letters (In). 1859–1866.
Letters From Bengal to the Resident. 1859–1863.
Governor's Letters to Bengal (Financial). 1862–1864.
Governor's Letters to Bengal (Judicial). 1862–1867.
Governor's Diary: General. 1858–1867.
Governor's Diary: Financial. 1858–1867.
Governor's Diary: Revenue. 1861–1866.
Government House: Guest Book. 1860–1867.
Government House: Office Attendance Register. 1860–1863.
Letters to Native Rulers. 1865–1872.

Straits Settlements Despatches. 1800–1872.
Despatches from Secretary of State to Straits Settlements. 1867–1915.
Despatches from Straits Settlements to Secretary of State. 1867–1915.
Despatches from Secretary of State to Straits Settlements. 1916–1941
Despatches from Straits Settlements to Secretary of State. 1916–1942
Register of Despatches to and from the Secretary of State. 1867–1940.
Index of Despatches to and from the Secretary of State. 1867–1922.
Confidential Despatches from Secretary of State to the Straits Settlements. 1861–1931.
Secret and Confidential Despatches to Secretary of State (Straits Settlements, Federated Malay States & Borneo). 1867–1931.
Register of Despatches, Secret and Confidential to and from Secretary of State. 1899–1941.
Federated Malay States High Commissioner's Despatches to Secretary of State (Including Schedules). 1897–1938.
Federated Malay States Despatches from Secretary of State to High Commissioner (Including Schedules). 1897–1940.

Academic Exercises
Saw, Chu Thong. "Transported Indian Convicts in Singapore, 1825–1873." Department of History, University of Malaya, Singapore, 1956.
Sinniah, Nasarathinam. "Government House, Singapore." Department of History, University of Malaya, Singapore, 1957.
Thio, Eunice. "The Singapore Chinese Protectorate: Events and Conditions leading up to its Establishment, 1823–1877." Department of History, University of Malaya, Singapore, 1952.

Drawings / Plans
Government House (Istana), IST 1–226. 1900–1945.

PRINTED MATERIALS
Legislative Council Proceedings
Straits Settlements Annual Reports. 1861–1952.
Straits Settlements, Federated Malay States and Unfederated Malay States Annual and Administration Reports. 1888–1949.
Straits Settlements Legislative Council Proceedings. 1867–1939.
Straits Settlements Executive Council Schedules. 1920–1939.
Straits Settlements Summary of Schedules. 1930–1936.
Straits Settlements Reference Books. 1904–1920.
Straits Settlements Circulars from Secretary of State. 1854–1915.
Straits Settlements Blue Books. 1870–1946.
Straits Settlements Legislative and Executive Council, Oaths of Office and Allegiance. 1867–1933.
Proceedings of the Federal Council of the Federated Malay States. 1909–1940.
Proceedings of the Advisory Council of the Malayan Union. 1946–1647.
Proceedings of the Legislative Council of the Federation of Malaya. 1948–1955.
Colony of Singapore Legislative Council Proceedings. 1948–1955.
Federal Legislative Council, Minutes and Council Papers and Debates. 1949–1959.
Straits Settlements Government Gazettes and Supplements. 1958–1941.
Municipal Fund of Singapore. 1880–1951.
Minutes of Proceedings of the Municipal Commissioners. 1952–1959.
Minutes of Proceedings of the City Council of Singapore. 1952–1959.
Hansard's Parliamentary Debates, Vol. 219–220. 1874.

Newspapers
Comrade. 1946.
The East. 1953.
Indian Daily Mail. 1946–1956.
Malayan Saturday Post. 1924–1933
Malayan Saturday Review. 1933–1934.
Malaya Tribune. 1914–1942.
Morning Tribune. 1936–1941, 1946–1962.
Singapore Daily News. 1932–1933.
The Singapore Daily Times. 1871–1876.
The Singapore Free Press. 1887, 1910–1942, 1946–1962.
Singapore Herald. 1939–1941.
The Singapore Standard. 1950–1959.
The Straits Observer, Singapore. 1874–1875.

Straits Times, Singapore. 1869-1999.
The Sunday Mirror. 1928-1929.
Syonan Shimbun. 1942-1945.

Journals

Mills, L. A. "British Malaya: 1824-1867." *Journal of the Malayan Branch Royal Asiatic Society*. Singapore, 1925.

Journal of the Malayan Branch Royal Asiatic Society, Vol. XXVI Part 1. Singapore, July 1953.

Quarterly Journal of the Institute of Architects of Malaya, Vol. IV No. 4. Singapore, 1955.

Books

Anson, Archibald Edward Harbord. *About Others & Myself: 1745-1920*. London: J. Murray, 1920.

Bastin, John, ed. *Travellers' Singapore: An Anthology*. Oxford in Asia Paperbacks. New York: Oxford University Press, 1994.

Begbie, P. J., Captain. *The Malayan Peninsula*. Kuala Lumpur: Oxford University Press, 1967.

Boulger, Demetrius Charles. *The Life of Sir Stamford Raffles*. Amsterdam: The Pepin Press, 1999.

Braddell, Roland St. John, Sir. *The Lights of Singapore*. London: Methuen, 1934.

Buckley, Charles Burton. *An Anecdotal History of Old Times in Singapore in 2 volumes*. Singapore: Fraser & Neave Ltd, 1902.

Cameron, Charlotte. *Wanderings in South Eastern Seas*. London: T. F. Unwin, 1924.

Chew, Melanie. *Leaders of Singapore*. Singapore: Resource Press, 1996.

Conrad, Joseph. *Youth; Heart of Darkness; The End of the Tether*. Edited with an introduction and notes by John Lyon. Penguin 20th Century Classics. London: Penguin Books, 1995.

Daljit Singh & Arasu, V.T., ed. *Singapore: An Illustrated History 1941-1984*. Singapore: Ministry of Culture Information Division, 1984.

Davies, Donald. *Old Singapore*. Singapore: D. Moore, 1954.
_____. *More Old Singapore*. Singapore: D Moore, 1956.

Earl, George Windsor. *The Eastern Seas*. With an introduction by C. M. Turnbull. Oxford in Asia Historical Reprints. Reprint of the 1837 ed. Singapore: Oxford University Press, 1971.

Friends of Singapore. *The House in Coleman Street*. Singapore: The Straits Times Press, 1956.

Gibson-Hill, Carl Alexander. *Notes on Government House*. Reprinted from the *Journal of the Malayan Branch of the Royal Asiatic Society*. Singapore: Malayan Branch Royal Asiatic Society, 1956.

Hahn, Emily. *Raffles of Singapore: A Biography*. London: Aldus Publications Ltd, 1948.

Hancock, T. H. H. *Coleman of Singapore*. London: Architectural Press, 1955.
_____, and C. A. Gibson Hill. *Architecture in Singapore*. With notes by T. H. H. Hancock and C. A. Gibson Hill on a collection of photographs by C. A Gibson. Singapore: Singapore Art Society Institute of Architects of Malaya, 1954.

Lee, Geok Boi. *Syonan: Singapore Under the Japanese 1942-1945*. Singapore: Singapore Heritage Society, 1992.

Lee, Kip Lin. *The Singapore House 1819-1942*. Singapore: Times Editions for Preservation of Monuments Board, 1988.

Lovat, Alice, Lady. *The Life of Sir Frederick Weld*. London: J. Murray, 1914.

Makepeace, Walter, Gilbert E. Brooke, and Roland St. J. Braddell, eds. *One Hundred Years of Singapore in 2 volumes*. Singapore: Oxford University Press, 1991.

McNair, John Frederick Adolphus. *Prisoners Their Own Warders*. Westminster: A Constable, 1899.

Montgomery, Brian. *Shenton of Singapore*. Singapore: Times Books International, 1984.

Onraet, Rene. *Singapore: A Police Background*. London: D. Crisp, [year unknown].

Pearson, H. F. *People of Early Singapore*. London: University of London Press, 1955.
_____. *Stories of Early Singapore*. London: University of London Press, 1954.

Raffles, Sophia. *Memoir of the Life and Public Services of Sir Thomas Stamford Raffles*. Oxford in Asia Hardback Preprints. Singapore: Oxford University Press, 1991.

Read, W. H. M. *Play and Politics: Reminiscences of Malays by an Old Resident*. London: W. Gardner & Darton, 1901.

de Silva, G. W. *Popular History of Malaya and The Netherlands Indies*. Kuala Lumpur: Kyle & Palmer, 1939.

Singapore Street Directory and Guide. Singapore, 1999.

Song, Ong Siang. *One Hundred Years' History of the Chinese in Singapore*. London: J. Murray, 1923.

Swettenham, Sir Frank Athelstane. *Footprints in Malaya*. London: Hutchinson & Co, 1942.

Vetch, Robert Hamilton, Colonel, ed. *The Life of Lieutenant-General The Honorary Sir Andrew Clarke. With a preface by Colonel Sir G. S. Clarke*. London: J. Murray, 1905.

Wilson, Margaret C. *Malaya: The Land of Enchantment*. Amersham: Mascot Press, [year unknown].

Wise, Michael, and Mun Him Wise, eds. *Travellers' Tales of Old Singapore*. Singapore, Times Books International, 1996.

Wurtzburg, C. E. *Raffles of the Eastern Isles*. London: Hodder & Stoughton, 1954.

MICROFILMS

Letters of The Extinguisher and Chronicles of St. George, University Library, Singapore.

India Public Despatch No. 6, paragraph 19. 8 September 1835.

ORAL HISTORY TRANSCRIPTS

Abdul Gaffor Bin Abdul Hamid, National Archives, Singapore.

AUDIO VISUAL RESOURCES

The Istana: The Jewel of the Temasek, Television Corporation of Singapore.
Hey Singapore!: Mysteries from the Istana, Television Corporation of Singapore.

MISCELLANEOUS MATERIALS

Documents and papers provided by the Office of the President including Day Book entries, information relating to the Istana ceremonial guards, the Istana household staff, the old furniture of the Istana, the bust of President Yusof Ishak, programmes of activities, official speeches, correspondence, memoranda and other miscellanea.

INDEX

Abdullah II bin Al-Hussein 133
Aide-de-camp 40, 85, 131
Ain Society 148
APSN Katong School 153, 155, 156, 157
Award ceremonies 134, 135, 136, 137, 138, 139, 140
Autism Association (Singapore) 157

Bendi, I Wayan 53, 54
Botanic Gardens 89
Boy Scouts 136
Boys' Brigade 135
Bukit Larangan (see Fort Canning)
Bukit Timah Road 19
Bush, George 85

Canning, Charles John 16
Cavenagh Road 19
Chan Khun Yew 54
Chinese Women's Association 125
Choo, Winston 40
Chua Mia Tee 54, 55, 139
Clarke, Sir Andrew 122
Clifford, Lady 89
Clifford, Sir Charles Hugh 89
Club Heal 148
Coleman, George D. 14
Commercial Square 14, 19
Council of Ministers 128
Crawfurd, John 16

Deng Xiaoping 85
Duchess of Somerset 17
Duke of Edinburgh 22, 104, 122

Edinburgh Road 101, 104, 105, 107
Empowering for Life Fund 152

Farquhar, Colonel William 14, 16
Forbidden Hill (see Fort Canning)

Fort Canning 12, 14, 16, 90

Gimson, Sir Franklin 30, 31, 33, 124
Girl Guides 134
Goh Chok Tong 62, 63, 140
Government House (old, pre-1959) 11, 12, 13, 14, 16, 17, 19, 21, 22, 23, 24, 25, 26, 28, 29, 30, 31, 33, 34, 35, 46, 89, 122, 123, 124, 125, 126, 127, 128
Guillemard, Sir Laurence Nunns 125, 126

Halimah Yacob 9, 110, 132, 133, 136, 137, 138, 139, 144, 145, 148, 149, 152, 153, 154, 155
HCSA Dayspring Residential Treatment Centre 157
Henderson, Sir Arthur 125
Hotel d'Europe 123

India 16, 46
Institute of Mental Health 149
Iskandar Shah, Raja 14

The Istana
    Banquet Hall 58, 59, 60, 61, 62, 63, 64
    Centre Gate 101, 104, 108
    Ceremonial Plaza 76, 114, 115, 129, 130
    Changing of Guards 101, 102, 103
    East Drawing Room 67, 68, 69, 71
    East Wing 46
    Entrance (to Main Building) 46, 49, 50, 51, 114, 115
    Entrance (to grounds) 101, 124
    Front Lawn 43, 48, 76, 88, 98, 99, 114, 115, 116, 117, 127
    Function Lawn (see Front Lawn)
    Garden Tours@Istana 145, 148, 150
    Golf course 89, 90
    Guardian of the House 24, 48, 52, 53, 100
    Gun Terrace 34
    Istana Art Event 144
    Istana Heritage Gallery 100, 145
    Istana Park 100, 101
    Istana Villa 78, 82, 83, 84, 85, 110, 130

Japanese Garden 41, 108, 109
Lily Pond 40, 58, 111, 112, 113
Main Building 35, 44, 45, 46, 47, 48, 50, 51, 78, 86, 98, 100, 114, 115, 118, 119, 130, 144, 145, 148, 159, 160
Main Gate 44, 100, 101, 102, 103, 107
Mandor statue (see Guardian of the House)
Open House days 9, 41, 88, 98, 100, 118, 119, 140, 144, 145, 146, 147, 148, 155
Picnic@Istana 148, 151
President's Lounge 76, 77
President's Personal Standard 35, 36, 37
Presidential Crest 35, 50, 51, 128
Queen Victoria Garden (see Lily Pond)
Queen Victoria Statue 58, 112
Reception Hall 56, 57
Sheares Room 54, 55, 72, 74, 75
Sri Melati 40, 78, 86
Sri Temasek 44, 78, 79, 80, 81, 82, 83
State Banquet 130, 134
State gifts 141, 142, 143
State Room 56, 57, 58
Swan Pond 106, 107, 148, 149
The Lodge 78, 86, 87
Visitors Book Room 101
Volunteer Gardeners@Istana 145, 150
West Drawing Room 72, 73, 130, 140
West Wing 58
Yusof Room 67, 68, 69

Japanese Occupation 10, 11, 29, 89, 101, 126
Java 26
Johor 26

Kampong Java Road 29
King George V (Prince George of Wales) 26, 124, 126

Lee Choon Guan 125
Lee Choon Guan, Mrs (see Tan Teck Neo)
Lee Kuan Yew 40, 110
Leembruggen, Jean 40
Lim Yew Kuan 54, 72

Mackenzie Road 124
Macmillan, Prime Minister Harold 128
Madras 26
Mahathir Mohamad 85
Malaysia 35, 40, 78, 128
McNair, John Frederick Adolphus 19, 21, 22
McNair Road 124
Melaka 16
Mount Sophia 19
Mountbatten, Lord Louis 33, 34, 128

Nair, C V Devan 86
Nathan, S R 54, 131, 141, 144, 152, 153

National Day, Singapore 100, 130, 160
National Museum Singapore 58
National Parks Board 89, 145
Nicoll, Sir John F 30
Niven, Laurence 89
North, Marianne 124

Ong Teng Cheong 24, 54, 63, 64, 86, 139
Orchard Road 19, 21, 44, 100, 101

Penang 16
Public Service Commission 34
President's Challenge 135, 145, 149, 152, 155
President's Scholarship 41, 135
Prince Albert Victor 26, 124
Prinsep, Charles Robert 16
Puan Noor Aishah 34, 41, 130, 134
Pulau Bukom Kechil 126
Pulau Seraya 126
Pulau Ubin 26

Queen Elizabeth II 126, 128

Raffles, Sir Stamford 12, 14, 16
Raffles Hotel 122

SG Enable 159
Sheares, Benjamin 72, 128, 130
Singapore Art Museum 144
Singapore Daily Times 22
Singapore Philatelic Museum 159
Song Ong Siang 126
Straits Settlements 16, 29, 30, 122, 125
Straits Times 122, 155
Sultan of Selangor 123

Tan Teck Neo 124, 125
Tan, Tony 98, 100, 110, 111, 139, 145, 146, 147, 152
Terauchi, Supreme Commander Count Hisaichi 29, 30, 126
Tojo, Prime Minister Hideki 126
TOUCH 159
Thomas, Sir Shenton 29

Vanda Miss Joaquim 95, 159
Victoria and Albert Museum 58

Wee Kim Wee, Dr 130
World War I 125
World War II 26, 46, 124, 128

Young, Sir Arthur 90, 125
Youth Corps Singapore 153
Yusof bin Ishak 34, 38, 39, 40, 41, 54, 67, 71, 74, 75, 78, 86

The Istana Main Building is often camouflaged in nature's abundance as befitting its position in a lush garden which is also a gazetted bird sanctuary.

THE ISTANA

Copyright 2019 © The Government of Singapore

First edition published in 2000; second edition published in 2011
This third edition published in 2019 on behalf of The Government of Singapore by:
Marshall Cavendish Editions, an imprint of Marshall Cavendish International (Asia)
1 New Industrial Road, Singapore 536196. Tel: (65) 6213 9300
Email: genrefsales@sg.marshallcavendish.com
Website: www.marshallcavendish.com/genref

All rights reserved. No part of this publication may be reproduced, stored in a retrieval system or transmitted, in any form or by any means, electronic, mechanical, photocopying, recording or otherwise, without the prior permission of the copyright owner. Requests for permission should be addressed to the Publisher.

Marshall Cavendish is a registered trademark of Times Publishing Limited

Text: K K Seet (first edition); Leong Ching (second edition); Hong Xinyi (third edition)
Photographs: Peter Mealin, unless otherwise stated in Image Credits
Marshall Cavendish Project Team: Glenn Wray, Melvin Neo, Bernard Go Kwang Meng

National Library Board, Singapore Cataloguing-in-Publication Data
Title: The Istana.
Description: Third edition. | Singapore : Published on behalf of The Government of Singapore by Marshall Cavendish Editions, 2019. | Previous edition: 2011. | Includes bibliographical references and index.
Identifier(s): OCN 1121162742 | ISBN 978-981-4868-91-4 (hardcover) | ISBN 978-981-4868-50-1 (paperback)
Subject(s): LCSH: Istana (Singapore). | Presidents--Dwellings--Singapore. | Official residences--Singapore. | Historic buildings--Singapore. | Singapore--Buildings, structures, etc.
Classification: DDC 725.17095957--dc23

Printed in Singapore